About th

Oscar Scafidi is an African political risk and security consultant, travel writer and international educator. Originally from the UK and Italy, he spent five years living and working in Luanda, Angola, between 2009 and 2014. Before this he was based in Khartoum, Sudan. Oscar's writing tends to focus on difficult destinations, such as Somalia, Afghanistan, Liberia and East Timor. In 2016 Oscar wrote the first ever English-language guidebook to Equatorial Guinea, having co-authored the second edition of the *Bradt Guide to Angola* in 2013. In July 2018 he released his new book, the *Bradt Guide to Angola* (third edition). He is currently based in Antananarivo, Madagascar.

KAYAK THE KWANZA

KAYAK THE KWANZA

OSCAR SCAFIDI

Unbound Digital

This edition first published in 2019

Unbound

6th Floor Mutual House, 70 Conduit Street, London W1S 2GF

www.unbound.com

All rights reserved

© Oscar Scafidi, 2019

The right of Oscar Scafidi to be identified as the author of this work has been asserted in accordance with Section 77 of the Copyright, Designs and Patents Act 1988. No part of this publication may be copied, reproduced, stored in a retrieval system, or transmitted, in any form or by any means without the prior permission of the publisher, nor be otherwise circulated in any form of binding or cover other than that in which it is published and without a similar condition being imposed on the subsequent purchaser.

All images are © Oscar Scafidi, unless otherwise specified.

ISBN (eBook): 978-1-78965-013-6

ISBN (Paperback): 978-1-78965-012-9

Cover design by Mecob

Printed and bound in Great Britain by Clays Ltd, Elcograf S.p.A.

Dear Reader,

The book you are holding came about in a rather different way to most others. It was funded directly by readers through a new website: Unbound.

Unbound is the creation of three writers. We started the company because we believed there had to be a better deal for both writers and readers. On the Unbound website, authors share the ideas for the books they want to write directly with readers. If enough of you support the book by pledging for it in advance, we produce a beautifully bound special subscribers' edition and distribute a regular edition and e-book wherever books are sold, in shops and online.

This new way of publishing is actually a very old idea (Samuel Johnson funded his dictionary this way). We're just using the internet to build each writer a network of patrons. Here, at the back of this book, you'll find the names of all the people who made it happen.

Publishing in this way means readers are no longer just passive consumers of the books they buy, and authors are free to write the books they really want. They get a much fairer return too – half the profits their books generate, rather than a tiny percentage of the cover price.

If you're not yet a subscriber, we hope that you'll want to join our publishing revolution and have your name listed in one of our books in the future. To get you started, here is a £5 discount on your first pledge. Just visit unbound.com, make your pledge and type KWANZA19 in the promo code box when you check out.

Thank you for your support,

Dan, Justin and John
Founders, Unbound

Super Patrons

Sheila Allan
Jordan Anderson
Matt Baines
Kevin Bartlett
Stephanie Bartlett
Mark Brighouse
Neil Chambers
Candice Cipullo
Regula Dannecker
Madison Earls
Chris Farquhar
Jonathan Finney
Jennifer Gagner
Peyton Gagner
Roma Giniyatov
Alasdair Glennie
Kim Gration
Jamie Green
Dennis Hadrick
The HALO Trust
Hannah Hamrick
Alex Handcock
Fiona Handcock
John Hilton
Benjamin Hodges
Jyoti Jaswal
Ishbel Macleod
Luis Miguel Pires
F Moss
Mark Newson
David Norris
José Pedro Agostinho, HALO Angola

João Piecho
Luis Piecho
Rita Piecho
Teresa Piecho
Laura Pollard
Chris Pym, HALO Angola
Francisco Quintino Ramos
David Reed
Sean Rorison
Alcides Safeca
Dario Scafidi
Jonathan Scafidi
Jack Schneider
Selina Shah
Dan Symons & Sarah Harding
System X Europe: Kayak Equipment Distribution
Carl Treeby
David True
Katy Jean Vance
Kristen VanOllefen
Voltaic Systems
Water-to-Go
Fidelity Weston
Ini Weston
Nick Wilski
Gerhard Zank, HALO Angola
Ben Zurawel

You are now at the crossing. And you want to choose, but there is no choosing there. There's only accepting. The choosing was done a long time ago.
    Cormac McCarthy, *The Counselor* (2013)

Contents

Foreword by Alfy Weston	xv
Preface	1
Alfy hatches a plan	5
Preparing for the expedition	9
Return to Luanda	19
Alone near the end of the world	27
The sinking	63
Rapids and hippos	89
Would you like to buy some diamonds?	117
Arrested at Capanda	139
Deportation	161
A covert expedition	171
Epilogue	183
Appendix 1 – A very brief history of Angola	187
Appendix 2 – Equipment list	195
Appendix 3 – Medical gear	199
Appendix 4 – Glossary and abbreviations	203
Patrons	205

Foreword by Alfy Weston

The mouth of the Kwanza River opens into the Atlantic just south of Angola's capital, Luanda. I spent many weekends on the river banks next to a fishing lodge perched on a spit of land at the mouth of the river. The waves of the Atlantic on one side and the flow of the river on the other. It was a spot that held my gaze and interest. Fishermen would come from afar to cast nets into the mouth of the river that was famed for its huge tarpon, other game fish and even tiger sharks. Great floats of exotic-looking reeds would drift down the river like giant flotillas, carrying snakes and birds. The river was constantly changing – some days it would flow gently by, on others there would be a great swell, and every now and then a storm would come and change the whole course of the river's mouth.

The Kwanza River caught my imagination. I began to do weekend expeditions from my home in Luanda to new places upstream. Before long, I had been to the main access points along the flat section of the river, which runs for 200km before it reaches the start of Angola's highlands. I had read about the importance of the river to the Portuguese colonisers and its use as a transport link for getting slaves to the coast. I had read the extraordinary tales of the eccentric British explorer Andrew Battel, who spent many years surviving as an outlaw on the lower section of the river in the sixteenth century. However, when my interest turned upriver into the highlands, there was remarkably little information to be found. The majority of the river had never been mapped and there was no record of anyone doing any substantial trip along its course.

I set about trying to find the source of the river. After some close examination on Google Earth, I identified what I thought to be the correct spot. One weekend, a friend and I set out to drive to the source. As we left Luanda that Saturday morning, I remember us feeling like intrepid explorers, setting out into the unknown. It was with some disappointment that after 1,500km of driving we found that the source of the river was sign-posted from the main road. However, the trip had shown us a route to access the source and I set about mapping the rest of the river using Google Earth and any local information I could find.

A few months later and I had all the information I needed to plan an expedition along Angola's longest river. The only thing I was missing was someone to do the trip with me. I immediately thought of Oscar. He had loved exploring the country and I knew he would be good company on long days of paddling. The only challenge was convincing him to leave his new job in London to spend six weeks in Angola. During a break from my work in Luanda, I arranged to meet Oscar on a wet, overcast day in the centre of London and he immediately took to the idea. Within a week, he'd handed in his notice and was committed. We would be out on the river within nine months.

We contacted the HALO Trust to find out more about the river near the source and associated mine risks. There is no organisation that knows this remote part of Angola better than the HALO Trust. The head of the HALO Trust in Angola, Gerhard Zank, met with me in Luanda. He had a keen sense of adventure and had just returned from motor biking solo along the Zambezi River. It was immediately reassuring to have his support. Gerhard was generous with his time and resources, and I soon learned more about the organisation he worked for. As we discovered more about the work they were doing in some of the most remote parts of Angola and the increasing struggle they have with funding, we decided to dedicate the trip to raising funds for a demining project. Whilst the initial intention to do the trip had been born out of curiosity and a sense of adventure, a great motivation became to complete it for the greater purpose of raising funds for the HALO Trust. During many long stretches of monotonous paddling, this proved to be the greatest incentive to keep going.

It was not just the HALO Trust that helped us with information about this remote African wilderness. Oscar has noted a long list of contributors to the success of this expedition, from conservationists to NGO workers and everything in between.

Oscar worked hard on recording the details of our trip, often scribbling away in his tent at the end of the day. This account is testament to the efforts he went to and the details that often passed me by.

Reading the book brought the whole expedition back to life for me, from the adrenaline rush of sinking in rapids to the chaos and confusion of being arrested in the middle of the night. I hope it will do the same for you.

Alfy Weston, Hong Kong, 18 October 2017

Preface

'Where are they? Down there?'

I was only half asleep when I heard these words, shouted in Portuguese. They came from further up the slope. Glancing at our luminous satellite-phone display, it was 12.30am. Far too late to be awake. We had to get up in less than six hours.

'Don't worry, *chefe*, we will get them out.'

Next came the unmistakable sound of a rifle being cocked, along with boot steps marching towards our tents. I immediately realised what was about to happen and rushed to get out of my sleeping bag. It was a freezing cold night and I did not want to be dragged out of my tent in just my boxer shorts. I had just pulled on my filthy cargo trousers when the zip of my tent was ripped open and in came the barrel of an AK-47 assault rifle. Beside it was a pair of hands, grabbing at me, waving handcuffs.

'Come out immediately!'

I tried to stall them while putting on my fleece. '*Calma*, I'm not going to run away!'

I thrust my bare feet out of the tent and pointed my soles up into the faces of the men staring down at me. This was not a pleasant sight. As had been my routine for the past nine days, prior to going to bed I had unwrapped my bandages and covered both pads with antiseptic cream. My feet were in a bad state from all the hiking with a heavy bag and the constant wet conditions. The combination of pus, blood and cream smeared across both feet made for a truly disgusting sight.

'He's injured, give him space.'

These instructions from the most senior member of the group meant they all stood back a few paces and let me put on some shoes. As soon as I stepped out of the tent, my hands were cuffed in front of me.

Ten metres to my left, Alfy was not faring so well in his tent. He had assumed that the men surrounding us were thieves here to steal our expedition gear and was resisting them. This was not an unreasonable assumption, given that nobody had identified themselves. Also, at least three of the seven armed men were wearing plain clothes. Alfy had grabbed the rifle barrel pointed into his tent, which resulted in him being hauled out, getting a knee in the back of the head and having his hands cuffed behind his back. It took a number of men to get him squashed face down on the floor and handcuffed. It sounded painful.

'Who are you and what do you want? Is it really necessary to have us handcuffed like this?'

I could now see that a few of the men were in uniform, and I directed my questions to the most senior-looking uniformed man.

'We are the Capanda Police Department, and you are under arrest for trespassing in a forbidden strategic site.'

'But we have all the necessary documentation, just check our bags!'

The police chief was having none of it. With a wave of his hand, our tents were pulled down with all of our gear still in them. Everything we owned, including our kayak, was thrown into the back of a waiting Toyota Land Cruiser. The official was particularly interested in our satellite phone, which he examined closely before handing it over to another member of the group. I became very apprehensive about him discovering our camera gear, but at least we did not have the drone any more.

The villagers, who had been eating fish with us only a few hours ago, stood around in shock as we were manhandled up the hill and put in the flatbed of the police 4×4. With our satellite phone confiscated, we had no way of informing anyone of our location. Then Alfy told me that they had neglected to take his mobile phone from him, as it was hidden in one of his trouser pockets.

'You will be spending the night with us at the police station.'

We drove off up the hill into the cold night air.

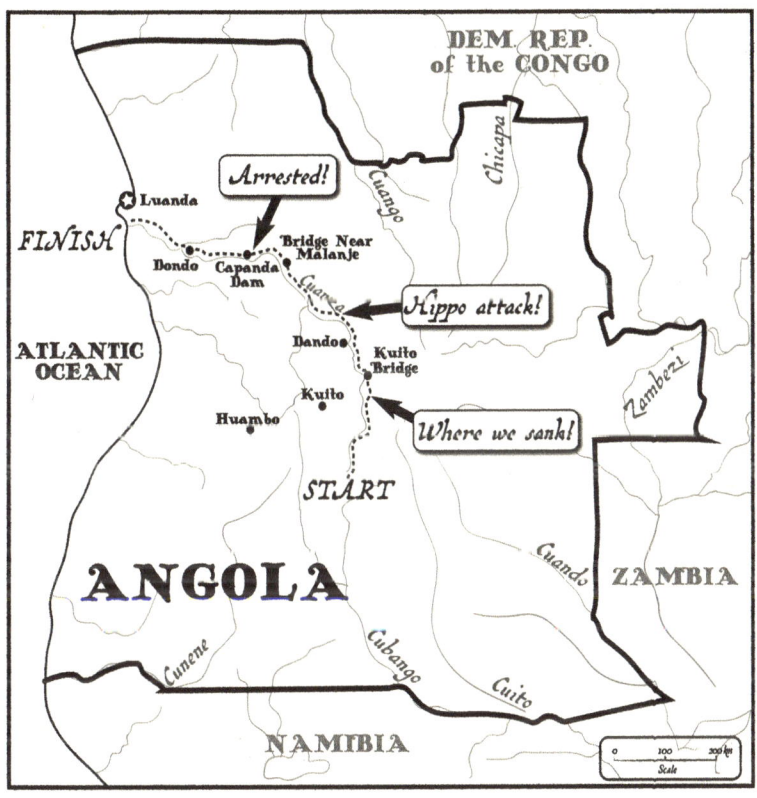

Figure 1 – Overview map of Angola. Image credit: Michael Peters

Alfy hatches a plan

In August 2009 I moved to Luanda, the Atlantic capital of Angola. I joined hundreds of thousands of Europeans who flooded into the country following the global financial crisis, hoping to earn a living in the booming oil-fuelled economy. These were heady years, following the end of Angola's 26-year civil war in April 2002. With the peace treaty signed, Angola now had an opportunity to exploit her vast reserves of natural resources, including proven offshore oil reserves (as of 2017, Angola is jockeying with Nigeria for the title of sub-Saharan Africa's largest oil exporter).

Despite living in Angola for five years, it is my British friend Alfy who must take the blame for the plan itself: to kayak the entire navigable length of the Kwanza River. Alfy and I met on the rugby pitch in Luanda in 2012 and became fast friends. He is a keen outdoorsman and was always coming up with new and exciting ways of exploring Angola. Tall, strawberry blonde, athletic and referred to by numerous female members of staff at my school as 'the one who looks like Prince Harry', Alfy had spent time living and working in Cameroon and East Timor before arriving in Angola.

Alfy's earlier attempts at expedition organisation in Angola should probably have served as a warning when it came to taking him up on his Kwanza River idea.

Once, in June 2014, he suggested that we walk the length of Mussulo, a 40km sand spit that juts into the Atlantic Ocean in front of Angola's capital city, Luanda. The journey was a three-day disaster, wading through knee-deep sand carrying all our own water and getting caught out in the open during a violent thunder storm one night. We set out on a Friday afternoon and completed the journey on Sunday morning, sleep deprived, covered in mosquito bites and very thankful we had not been struck by lightning.

In October 2014, Alfy, along with his visiting brothers, spent one of his holidays kayaking from Kambambe Dam (near Dondo) to Luanda, which involved paddling 220km of the Kwanza River's lower course, then 80km north up the Atlantic coastline. This was his first

Figure 2 – Walking the length of Mussulo (June 2014)

time testing out his prized Klepper collapsible kayak on the river, and it led him to wonder whether the journey could be scaled up to cover the whole course.

Klepper is a German brand of collapsible kayak, first built in the 1940s. Alfy's vessel was slightly newer, having first been assembled in the 1960s, but it was the same basic idea: collapsible wooden skeleton, canvas skin, room for two paddlers. German navigator Dr Hannes Lindemann had used exactly the same model (Aerius II) to cross the Atlantic Ocean solo in 1956. Special Forces worldwide, including US Navy SEALs, continue to use the Klepper kayak to this day due to its lightweight design, portability and rugged build.

Alfy first seriously suggested the expedition to me in an email in October 2014, only a few months after I had left Angola to return to London for work.

21 Oct 2014

Hey Oscar,

How's life? Kambambe Dam to Luanda kayak trip

completed. Did it with my two brothers and a friend three weeks ago. Great trip. I actually don't have a single photo but my brother took some and says he'll do a video which I will forward through.

I really think we could do the whole river. The whole Kwanza journey would be around July time and I think take two months. I also think it needs to be recorded in some way.

I had left Angola in July 2014 to move to London and was already very keen to head back and visit my old home. However, the timing was not great for a 2015 start date.

29 Oct 2014
Hey Alfy,
Kayak trip with your brothers sounds epic! Did you have any trouble from the authorities? Were the fishermen confused seeing you paddle down the river? I really don't think I can do July 2015 as a start date due to work commitments here in London. However, if we shoot for June / July 2016, that gives us over 20 months to prepare. That has to be enough time to get everything in order, surely?

Our messages went back and forth for many months. Work schedules continued to get in the way. It was not until October 2015 that we finally both committed to the journey.

12 Oct 2015
Oscar, I think the best canoe option would be something collapsible and lightweight like a pack raft. There are a fair number of waterfalls that we would need to walk around including a 200km slog at one point. My challenge is that I won't be able to commit to it until much nearer the time as it will need me to negotiate time off before starting my next posting which will only be announced in May 2016.

13 Oct 2015
Hey Alfy,
This sounds more and more epic. A 200km trek? Sign me up! Those raft packs are expensive, but I guess if we could secure some sponsorship it might be better.

There's no way I can wait until May 2016 to find out whether the trip is happening or not. It'll take months of preparation, likely starting in January. Would your work be more flexible and more willing to give you the time off, if you presented it as a *fait accompli*, with sponsorship in place? Do you think your work would be more open to it if we made it a charity trip too? I know the HALO Trust could definitely do with some publicity and donations at the moment!

Meanwhile, you have a look into the exact route we would be navigating, how much of this is practical and any safety concerns. It would also be useful to have a more exact estimate of when we could start (I'm flexible on that one) and how long it would take, as this is the sort of thing sponsors are bound to ask. Either way: I'm in!

Timing-wise, a projected start date of June 2016 worked perfectly for both of us: Alfy had a gap between finishing his job in Angola and starting a new role in Hong Kong, and I also had a work contract coming to an end in March 2016.

We both committed.

Preparing for the expedition

How you prepare to kayak and hike 1,300km through the African bush is dependent upon where you live. Alfy was still in Luanda, whereas I was stuck in London, with no opportunities to travel until the expedition started. We were both also relative novices when it came to kayaking. Alfy at least had the 300km journey from back in October 2014 under his belt. I, on the other hand, had only been sea-kayaking in Cornwall once and done a few afternoons paddling on Ardingly Reservoir in West Sussex. Given our very different locations and schedules in the nine months prior to the trip, we divided up the expedition logistics as sensibly as possible, then set about training for the task ahead.

Figure 3 – Alfy and his brothers on the Kwanza River (October 2014)
Image credit: Alfy Weston

Alfy was still based in Angola, working for a company called Swire Serviços Maritimos Ltd, part of the massive Swire conglomerate. He was country manager and, as far as I could make out, it was his job to organise and monitor service ships going out to oil rigs.

As well as his office role, Alfy had one of the most important jobs on the expedition: mapping out our route. He did this through a combination of speaking to local sources, reviewing notes from his previous trip, site visits and poring over satellite photography of the River Kwanza. He came up with a system for grading rapids based on their difficulty: one was OK to paddle down, two was marginal, three and above meant we would likely be doing some portage around them (which is a technical term for carrying the bloody kayak). This was a difficult call to make based in some cases solely on Google Earth's out-of-date photographs. For longer sections that were not navigable, Alfy had to find an accessible hiking route around them (bearing in mind we would be carrying all of our gear and the dismantled Klepper).

He also needed to take note of potential emergency evacuation routes for each day. In most cases this meant getting to the nearest track where a 4×4 could reach us. In some very isolated sections, it meant finding dirt strips for a bush pilot to land on. No matter how carefully he planned, help was going to be a very long way away if things went wrong.

Alfy also worked out where we could meet up with a 4×4 from the HALO Trust for supply drops along the way. Gerhard Zank, the HALO Trust's Programme Manager for Angola, was very excited to hear about our proposed expedition and keen to help make it a success. He and his team would be instrumental in us completing the trip.

Alfy budgeted us between 50 and 60km of kayaking on a good day with no obstacles, or at least 20km of hiking. These distances were based on his earlier kayaking trip along the Kwanza, and on paper did not sound too difficult. We had the river divided into three sections for the expedition. The first section ran from the source up to what we called Kuito Bridge, near the mining town of Camacupa. It was very isolated, but as far as we could tell, there were not too many obstacles. The second section, running from Camacupa to Capanda Dam, was full of rapids and waterfalls and would involve a lot of portage. To get to the third section, starting at Dondo, would initially involve a hike past two hydroelectric dams, then it was a clear 220km of paddling to the finish. This was going to be by far the easiest section, as there are no hippos, rapids or waterfalls on the lower stretches of the Kwanza and Alfy had kayaked this section before in 2014. (*See the Overview Map on p. 3.*)

Another important task was navigating the Angolan bureaucracy and securing us all the necessary permits for the expedition. Alfy was far better placed to do this than I was, given his location and resultant access to the relevant ministries. The Angolan ministries are notoriously difficult to interact with, and ours was a very unusual request. From a legal standpoint, we should not have needed any permits: Alfy had a work visa and I would enter the country with whichever visa the Angolan Embassy in London said was most suitable (likely a tourist visa). Both these visas should allow full access to the entire country, including the river.

In reality, we both knew this is not how things work in Angola. We were bound to encounter overly officious security forces on our travels and thought it better to pre-empt their requests by getting the trip approved by someone important. Exactly who to ask was a bit of a mystery though. In the end, Alfy hedged his bets and got us permits from the Ministry of Environment, Ministry of Tourism and Ministry of Water and Energy, as well as notifying the relevant provincial authorities.

We thought this, along with our visas and letters of introduction from the HALO Trust, would be sufficient paperwork for even the most fastidious officials.

Through Osvaldo, his local business partner in Luanda, Alfy got our trip signed off by a variety of important-sounding people. Osvaldo's networking skills were quite a thing to behold: we needed a permit? He had a cousin in the ministry. We were not sure of the name of the person we needed to approach? Osvaldo would make a few calls. Time and again, he came through for us, saving Alfy a lot of time and effort in the process.

Our permit from the Ministry of Water and Energy, running to an impressive six pages, was incredibly detailed, outlining exactly who we were, what we were doing and why. It even talked about the specifics of our route and plans for camping! With this level of organisation, what could possibly go wrong?

While Alfy was running around route-planning and getting us permits, I was busy sourcing the kit we required for the expedition. Keeping things light and compact was key: not only would we need to be able to pack it all into the Klepper and kayak along with it, but we would also have to carry it for long sections of the trip. My aim was to keep both of our hiking packs below 25kg (without water). Cost was also a big factor, as we were self-funding the entire expedition on a very tight budget.

After expending a lot of time and energy trying to persuade gear manufacturers to sponsor us, I realised that very few companies were willing to take a gamble on two unproven commodities, especially on such a risky journey. There were a few happy exceptions though: we managed to get water filtration bottles from Water-to-Go, carbon-fibre paddles from Werner Paddles and a battery and solar-panel setup from Voltaic Systems that we could use to charge our electronics while on the move.

The rest, such as camping equipment, medical supplies, communications and navigation gear came out of our own pocket. A full list of our gear can be found in Appendix 2, but Figure 4 shows a few of our favourite items from the trip, including the Trangia cooking system, the lethal-looking Camillus X Carnivore machete, the LED Lenser SEO7R Rechargeable Li-ion Head Torch and the Icebreaker Merino wool base layer that saved us from hypothermia on more than one occasion!

A fair amount of the budget was also eaten up by filming equipment, including a DJI Phantom 3 drone (for panoramic shots of the landscapes). Alfy and I both agreed that despite the extra weight and cost, filming the trip would do wonders for public interest, thus helping to drive up donations to the HALO Trust. We were also keen on preserving the memories of this unique expedition on film.

One area where we managed to save money was organising the food. Rather than fork out hundreds of pounds on freeze-dried expedition rations, I bought a dehydrator and vacuum sealer and made most of the meals myself.

Preparing for the expedition

Figure 4 – 25kg of expedition gear

My flat in Kennington, south London, which I shared with my long-suffering girlfriend Steph, soon became ground zero for experimental dehydration recipes. The living room and open-plan kitchen were small, but luckily we had large bay windows, which could be thrown open to air out the flat anytime anything went wrong.

Making dehydrated expedition rations is a slow affair. First, you need to cook the food as you would normally. Then you have to spread it out over a series of permeated trays, which you place into the dehydrator – essentially a big drying rack with a motor at the bottom, like a hairdryer. A few hours later, all the moisture has evaporated and you have a lightweight, portable food source.

My girlfriend, Steph, soon got used to coming home to our flat to the smell of sweet potato, tuna or kidney beans slowly drying out in the kitchen. Tuna in particular was not a popular choice, as even with the bay windows open, there was no escaping the fishy smell.

I dehydrated enough supplies to last us a month with no outside contact, which was more than enough. Then I vacuum-sealed the food in individual servings using another fancy piece of kit ordered from Amazon. Sharp items, such as dehydrated seafood sticks, posed a particular challenge as they could pierce the plastic coating and ruin the vacuum seal for that portion. Unsealed rations were no use to us, as they would allow in moisture and bacteria, risking spoilage during the expedition.

We knew that we could probably buy fish from local fishermen as we navigated the river (assuming we saw any) but other than that, we needed to be self-reliant for our calorie intake. With a lot of experimentation and a few comments from the neighbours, we soon had all the dehydrated food we needed to survive in the Angolan bush.

I also fired up our digital marketing campaign. We settled on an aim to raise ten thousand dollars for the HALO Trust, which was enough to pay for one month of work by a demining team down in Cuito Cuanavale, sadly known as Africa's most landmined town. This money would help clear around 4,000m^2 of minefields, which could then be returned to the local community for use.

Ten thousand dollars sounded like a nice round number, but we had no idea if it was achievable. To get anywhere close to that figure, we needed to publicise our journey as far and wide as possible.

I had a little bit of experience using Twitter to publicise a travel guide to Equatorial Guinea that I wrote in 2015, but it was still a steep learning curve. Despite this, by November 2015 we had a well-established Twitter and Facebook presence, as well as our own JustGiving page, website (www.kayakthekwanza.com) and blog (www.kayakthekwanza.wordpress.com). We even managed to get ourselves featured in three magazines before we set out.

> **Why do the HALO Trust need help?**
> Between 1975 and 2002 over 20 million landmines were planted during the Angolan Civil War. There is great wealth originating from Angola's abundant natural resources which could be used to deal with this problem, but this wealth is distributed highly unevenly.
>
> Angola had the fifth largest economy in Africa in 2015 according to the World Bank, yet that same year UNICEF highlighted it as the country with the highest infant mortality rates in the world, with one in six Angolan children dying before the age of five. Seventy per cent of the population live on less than two US dollars per day and the World Health Organization (WHO) stated life expectancy as 51 years for men in 2015. Angola was ranked in the bottom six nations in Transparency International's 2015 Corruption Perceptions Index.
>
> These economic disparities cause many problems for the people of Angola – and those attempting to help them. The country's rapid graduation to upper middle-income levels means that donors and international organisations are far less willing to provide financial assistance to the government, reasoning that they are wealthy enough to pay for development projects themselves. Other donors are concerned that funds or budgetary assistance may be siphoned off by corrupt officials rather than helping to develop the country. NGOs such as the HALO Trust have seen their donations from Organisation for Economic Cooperation and Development governments slashed, with no corresponding increase in levels of government support. Donald Trump's election in November 2016, with his pledges to slash discretionary federal funding to the State Department and foreign aid programmes, has not helped the situation.

We also decided to speak to Guinness World Records about having our expedition recognised as a world first. Great recognition if we managed to finish, but also another way of getting the public interested in our journey. According to the requirements of Guinness World Records, we needed to paddle, roll and carry the Klepper under our own steam the entire length of the Kwanza for our first descent of the Kwanza to count as a record. We also needed to keep detailed logs of our progress each day. This all sounded pretty straightforward.

All of this publicity was great for driving traffic to the JustGiving site and encouraging donations, but it also piled on the pressure. We had created a lot of expectation around the trip. What if we failed to complete it?

The most important part of our preparations was to get our bodies ready for the task in front of them. Alfy and I did things a little differently in this regard. Being London-based, I immediately joined a kayaking club on the River Thames, called the London Kayak Company. Their clientele are mainly tourists who want to get a different view of London by paddling west along the river from Cutty Sark to Tower Bridge or sometimes Vauxhall. Of the four or five kayak companies I contacted to ask for help, they were the only ones who sent back a positive response. Having read their founder's kayaking CV, I am not at all surprised.

Harry Whelan set a world record in 2011 by circumnavigating Ireland in a blisteringly fast 25 days, covering 1,000 miles. In 2005 he was part of a three-man team that circumnavigated Great Britain in 80 days. Our jaunt along the Kwanza was right up his street. So, under the tutelage of Harry's business partner Gavin McEachran, in April 2016 I headed out onto the freezing cold River Thames, trying my hardest not to capsize or swallow any water. I also completed a whitewater safety and rescue swimming course at Lee Valley White Water Centre.

Alfy had access to the Klepper kayak and to the Kwanza River, so his training could be a little more representative of what we were actually going to face. However, like me, he had a full-time job getting in the way of his training. If we had known then what we know now about the challenges we would face, our training regimes would have been far more rigorous. The spring passed quickly and soon it was time to jump on a plane and join Alfy in Angola.

PREPARING FOR THE EXPEDITION

Figure 5 – Kayaking on London's River Thames (May 2016)

Return to Luanda

I left Angola in July 2014, when oil was at $107 per barrel and they were pumping out 1.7 million barrels per day, making it Africa's second largest exporter after Nigeria. Ninety-five per cent of total exports and 80 per cent of government revenue came from selling oil and there were few efforts to diversify away from this one-dimensional extractive model. This was a risky strategy, as the global oil price is notoriously volatile. When I stepped off the plane for our kayak expedition in June 2016, oil had plummeted to forty-six dollars per barrel.

The global drop in oil prices had devastated Angola's economy. For the first time, foreigners arriving in Angola with US dollars found it cheap: the official exchange rate was 165 kwanzas to the dollar, but rampant inflation and a liquidity crisis had pushed the black-market rate up to six hundred kwanzas per dollar. The cost of living skyrocketed for the Angolan people as imports became more and more expensive.

I touched down in Luanda on 31 May and already had a presentation to give at Luanda International School (LIS) the next day. The staff, students and parents had really got behind our expedition and raised thousands of dollars in donations before we had even started. The LIS Global Issues Network were particularly impressive, handing me a home-made oversize cheque for three hundred thousand kwanzas (about $1,800 at the official exchange rate), raised through various fundraising initiatives over the previous five months.

I gave a number of talks to the student body between 1 June and 3 June, explaining what we were doing and why. The Primary students in particular were fascinated, if a little confused.

'What happens if you get eaten by a crocodile?' asked one particularly concerned seven-year-old.

'What if you fall off a waterfall?' asked another.

By the end of the Q&A session Alfy and I had been hypothetically killed by water, disease, hippos, crocodiles, lions and all manner of beasts that do not even live along the Kwanza River.

I delivered some platitudes to the crowd about our medical kit and emergency evacuation plan, but had to concede that it would be a major problem if one of us got eaten by a wild animal along the way. One Secondary student also pointed out the potential irony of stepping on a landmine while on an expedition raising money for landmine removal. We were, after all, travelling through remote parts of Angola that had been seriously affected by the civil war. I could not help but laugh.

While I was busy on the public relations trail, Alfy was still at work, making the final arrangements for vanishing into the bush for a month. His work calendar was the driving force behind the strict schedule we were on: if setting out in early June, he needed to be back in Luanda by Monday 11 July in order for him to return to work and organise a handover with his replacement as country manager. His schedule actually had us starting hiking on 5 June and crossing the finish line into the Atlantic Ocean exactly a month later on 5 July, so we had almost a week of leeway for unexpected delays. Which was lucky, because as it turned out, there were a *lot* of unexpected delays.

While working a full-time job Alfy also had to chase down the final few pieces of paperwork we required from his local partner and discuss plans with his driver, Garcia, for potential resupply drops on the lower sections of the Kwanza (which are more easily accessible from Luanda). Looking at the map, it seemed that Garcia and his 4×4 could not access us at any stage before we reached Malanje Bridge, which represented the start of the last third of the expedition.

Garcia was such a positive influence, even at this early stage. He was Alfy's right-hand man at the company. Short, muscular, with cropped hair and always sporting a pair of the latest shades, Garcia was very much a man of action. Having started in the role of driver, he had, through great persistence, graduated to taking on a number of different responsibilities. Dressed in smart trousers and always wearing a collared shirt, he was there smiling, waiting for me at Quatro de Fevereiro Airport when I landed and was just as enthusiastic (if a little exhausted) at the end of our trip. Visitors landing at Luanda's international airport will note that the name translates as Fourth of February, which many assume to be the independence date. In fact, it marks the beginning of the anti-colonial struggle that the Angolans fought against Portuguese occupation, beginning in 1961.

We spent the first few frantic evenings in Alfy's flat laying out all the kit, checking and rechecking that everything was in working order. Alfy's girlfriend, Marie-Louise, was not particularly impressed that the living room now looked like a boat yard but she was incredibly supportive of the whole endeavour. Marie-Louise, also British, had a background in education and worked for an NGO in Angola. She and Alfy had been together since their undergraduate days at Cambridge University. Petite, with long brown hair, and cheerful, she cooked us some epic meals on those last few nights in civilisation, to prepare us for the leaner times ahead. On 2 June the three of us had our last meal together in the Luanda flat, before setting off for Huambo early the next morning.

The internal flight from Luanda to Huambo took just over an hour. At the time, the national carrier, TAAG, had a poor reputation for domestic flights. Having said this, things have certainly changed a lot from TAAG's chaotic early post-war days. On 25 May 2003 one of TAAG's leased aircraft, a Boeing 727-223, was stolen from its parking spot at Luanda's Quatro de Fevereiro Airport, right under the air-traffic controllers' noses. To this day, the mystery of who took it or where it went remains unsolved.

Flying southeast from the capital, we were heading inland to Huambo, the largest city on the Bié Plateau, to the headquarters of the HALO Trust. Their reason for being in Huambo? This was one of the most fiercely fought-over cities during the civil war and a key base for the rebel UNITA movement, one of the main protagonists in both the war of independence (1961–1974) and the civil war (1975–2002). In fact, the three contenders for political control in post-independence Angola were all movements that had fought Portuguese rule for many years: the FNLA, MPLA and UNITA.

The executed UNITA leader Jonas Savimbi's burned-out house still sits abandoned on one of the main roads. The remaining shell of the structure, with a spiral staircase, hints at the former luxury of this residence. It was known locally as the *Casa Branca* (the white house). In a 1986 diplomatic trip to meet President Ronald Reagan in

Washington, Savimbi is purported to have joked that 'he had a White House too'. Those days are long past now, but the effects of the fighting can be seen everywhere: bullet holes in the concrete walls, whole buildings collapsed in on themselves from artillery fire. The hinterland is still infested with landmines, which affect the local farming communities.

The city of Huambo sits at an elevation of 1,700m and was favoured by the Portuguese during colonial times for its cooler temperatures, predictable rainfall and excellent farmland. There was even talk of making it the colonial capital at one stage, but the lack of a port was a problem. It was originally the centre of the Ovimbundu Kingdom of Wambu, founded by Ngola Ciluanji, the son of Feti, who was the first ever man in the Ovimbundu creation story.

As we drove down the tree-lined boulevards past the war-scarred cityscape, it was like stepping back in time. Portuguese writer and director Miguel Hurst has called this style of colonial architecture 'an agglomeration of Tropical and Brazilian Modernisms with European styles inherited from the likes of Le Corbusier'. I thought it all looked like something out of The Jetsons – a US cartoon programme produced in the early 1960s, but designed to look futuristic. Huambo was quite affluent back in the 1950s and 1960s, but today the combination of natural decay and war damage give it an eerie feel.

The HALO Trust has their staff headquarters opposite the main hospital in town. It was here that we met Harriet, who at the time of our arrival was the only HALO Trust staff member staying in the house. It is a large building, also known as the *Casa Branca* (white house) to locals – not to be confused with the other *Casa Branca* in town, which is Savimbi's former residence. Large, airy and with a generous back garden featuring a number of outbuildings and even a wood-fired pizza oven, this building was the centre of the large expatriate NGO community present in the city during the civil war. At one stage in the '90s it was home to up to 30 HALO staff, including many from other landmine-affected countries such as Eritrea. Today it was just Harriet from the UK.

Harriet's official title was Projects Officer. An experienced NGO worker, she had already lived and worked in Colombia before being

Figure 6 – Ruins of Savimbi's Casa Branca (March 2014)

posted to Angola. She gave us the grand tour and showed us where we would be sleeping for the night, before setting out for the source of the Kwanza the next day. Harriet also drove us out to the HALO Trust headquarters on the outskirts of town, to pick up the satellite phones we would be using throughout the journey. Here we were given a tour of the equipment used for demining and shown a display of the unexploded ordnance (UXO) collected from the surrounding countryside. There were landmines from Egypt, China, Cuba, South Africa, as well as various rocket-propelled grenades, mortars and other devices. It seemed that most countries' weapons industries had not been shy about fuelling the carnage during the long civil war.

Alfy and I took this layover in Huambo as an opportunity to check all the gear one last time and ensure nothing was damaged during the flight from Luanda. Luckily, the only casualty was my bottle of

Figure 7 – Landmines and UXO made safe by the HALO Trust in Huambo (April 2012)

tabasco sauce, which made for a month of bland meals out on the river.

While unpacking gear in his room, Alfy expressed some concern at the total weight of the kit we were packing up and also something we had not worried about up until this point: the volume. All of our bags needed to be either strapped to the back of the kayak or pushed inside the hollows in the front and back sections of the skin. At its widest, the kayak was only 86cm. Some of our bags were already bulging out to beyond this point, but all we could do was unload some non-essentials and contend with the rest later. That evening we had more important things to deal with, namely a last supper and beers in town.

Our options for food were pretty limited, so we settled on a Portuguese joint that did simple meat and fish dishes. It was a good opportunity to get to know Harriet a bit better. After all, she would be our first point of contact while on the expedition. If we didn't check in one night on the satellite phone, then it was her job to implement the emergency plans.

'So how has life been down here in Huambo? Much going on?'

I had been down here on a number of trips, and while the city had a faded colonial charm, I could not imagine living there.

'Well, work keeps us pretty busy. We've been testing out drones for mine detection recently, which is exciting! Other than that, there really isn't much to do in your free time. Knitting, reading, watching DVDs. I got mugged walking back from the restaurant a few months ago, which is probably the most exciting thing to happen to a HALO Trust person down here in years.'

Alfy seemed incredulous. From what we had both heard, the city was extremely safe.

'What happened? Were you hurt?'

'No, not really.'

Harriet seemed very matter of fact about the whole affair.

'He just pushed me over and grabbed my purse. I hit my head but nothing too serious. Anyway, I can't wait to get out of here. My next posting starts soon. I'm heading back to Colombia, where I worked previously.'

'Yes, Colombia has to be a bit livelier than down here.'

I sipped my Coke and wondered how long I would cope in an isolated posting like this one. The spartan lifestyle Harriet was living down in Huambo made me feel guilty about the excesses of my previous expatriate life in Luanda. The house Harriet lived in was beautiful, in a dusty colonial sort of way, but there was not much to do.

Alfy was very keen to discuss logistics, and Harriet seemed genuinely interested.

'So how far do you think you will travel every day? Do you have an exact plan?'

'That's what Oscar keeps asking me! I've mapped it out in a fair bit of detail. We need to be hitting at least 50km of paddling per day to stay on track. For walking days, we're aiming for 20km, but this varies depending on the terrain. Getting out of the river and in again is a hassle, so hopefully there won't be too much portage.'

We discussed our plans for the journey in the quiet restaurant while shovelling down as much steak and potato as possible. One of the few positive influences of the Portuguese in Angola was on the cuisine: they really know how to do steak! Chunky, medium rare and slathered in peppercorn sauce with an egg on top, we would not taste anything this good again for at least six weeks.

This was potentially my last opportunity to have a beer for a month, but for some reason I was not thirsty. We all went to bed very full and very apprehensive that night.

Alone near the end of the world

The first day of the expedition was Sunday, 5 June 2016. Whatever anxiety had built up over the past six months of preparation seemed to melt away on the first morning of the expedition. Finally, it was here. The reason I had been dodging ferries on the Thames, eating weird food, obsessing about our social media 'presence' and jumping through hoops for the Angolan bureaucracy. Earlier on in the week I had stood in front of hundreds of students and former work colleagues and boldly predicted that Alfy and I would be the first people to successfully navigate the Kwanza River from source to sea. Now it was time to actually do it.

After a quick test of the drone we loaded up one of the 4x4s, a trusty old Land Rover Defender, and set out for the source of the Kwanza. We were accompanied by Valdemar Gonçalves Fernandez (HALO's Programme Operations Officer) and driven by Francisco Manuel Catimba. Both these men had experience of helping foreigners undertake expeditions in remote parts of Angola: they had been part of National Geographic's Okavango Wilderness Project support team the previous year.

Like many of the HALO Trust employees in this part of the world, Valdemar had a hint of the military about him. Dressed in khaki combat trousers, a HALO Trust cap and the type of multi-pocketed vest you see photographers dashing about war zones in, the only thing scruffy about him was his beard. We headed south-east from Huambo, out into the Angolan highlands. The further we drove, the more isolated it became. We were the only vehicle on the road for long periods of the final hour. We were reassured by Valdemar's understated enthusiasm for the expedition, as he told us that he had already spoken to the local communities on the first stretch.

'They are expecting you. We work closely with the authorities in this region, and all the people know us. There should be no problems for you while you are hiking.'

Oddly enough, the source is actually marked with a brown tourist information sign from the main road. I cannot imagine they get many tourists down here though. We turned right and set out over a boggy mud track, getting the Land Rover stuck on a crude log bridge over a stream. The source itself was a bit of an anti-climax: a large depression with waist-high grass, surrounded by forest on every side. There were a series of sticks stuck into the bog to designate the source. The path leading down to the water looked well used.

Although we could not see it, Valdemar told us that there was a village a few kilometres away that collected water here. Given that it was already late afternoon, the HALO team decided to spend the night there. That way they could see us off in the morning and remind the local population to expect two foreigners dragging a large buggy over the next two days! We took a sombre team photo and then off they went. Alfy and I were finally on our own.

We hiked a kilometre or so up a hill and set up camp. There were cultivated fields on both sides of the path, which I found reassuring. At this stage, people were not that far away if we needed them. We were both still blissfully ignorant of the degree of challenge we had taken on, but Angola was about to let us know very quickly.

That first night proved problematic for both Alfy and me, and for similar reasons. Getting accurate weather data for the Angolan highlands had proven difficult in the run-up to the expedition. The nearest weather station, over in Kuito, told us that night-time temperatures went down to around seven degrees Celsius in this part of Angola at this time of year. We were foolish to trust such a distant source of weather data, as that night it quickly dropped to below zero. Alfy struggled to stay warm in his two-season sleeping bag and even my three-season was not exactly toasty warm. Our Merino wool base layers were put to immediate good use.

My issues were more mechanical than atmospheric: my tent had a manufacturing flaw that meant it was not fully taut when put up. This reduced the interior size of the tent to smaller than my height. I had used this model of tent before and chose it because of its light weight. However, this was a brand-new tent that I had picked up in London and I had not thought to actually put it up before flying to Angola. Instead I had simply unpacked it and checked all the parts were there. From night one I had the option: sleep in the foetal position or stretch out, touch my feet against the lining and gradually get them wet as water seeped in. I tried both over the course of the month, cursing my tent every time.

Before falling asleep, Alfy filmed the first of many diary-cam entries. We had agreed beforehand that this would be the easiest format to record our thoughts in, as nobody wanted to be writing detailed journals every night. The plan was to try and state some logistical information about our progress, then reflect on how we were feeling that day. We got the idea from watching Ewan McGregor and Charley Boorman's excellent *Long Way Round* documentary, about their 2004 motorbike trip from London to New York. It took about four days for this plan to go out the window. We were simply too exhausted most nights to say anything useful into a camera. Our filming became more and more intermittent as the journey went on.

While Alfy was reflecting on the day, I used the satellite phone to text our position to three different people: Harriet, back in Huambo (for safety), my brother Jonathan, back in Edinburgh (who had kindly agreed to live-update our Twitter feed) and the automatic tracking map for our website, so followers could follow our progress in real time. Jonathan, three and a half years my junior, was busy studying for his Masters at Edinburgh University. He had plenty of experience of my hare-brained travel schemes: back in 2010 he and I drove a 1980s Volkswagen Transporter van from London to Russia and back again, via the breakaway Republic of Abkhazia. It was good to know that he would be following along and looking out for us on this latest adventure.

That night, I thought back to the last time I had been in a part of Angola this remote, on a research trip. In fact, it had been only a few hundred kilometres to the south-east of the spot where we were camping, in a place called Cuito Cuanavale, a small settlement in Cuando Cubango Province. In 2012 I had the opportunity to co-author the second edition of Bradt Travel Guides' tourist guidebook on Angola. This meant visiting and documenting all 18 provinces in Africa's seventh largest country. It was what I saw on this journey that originally convinced me that the HALO Trust was the most suitable charity to support through our expedition.

The Portuguese colonists used to call Cuando Cubango *terra do fim do mundo* (land at the end of the world) due to its remote location and poor communication links. However, the local population no longer use this pejorative designation. Cuito Cuanavale took on new significance during the Angolan Civil War as the site of a huge land battle, which pitted Western-supported UNITA troops against the communist-backed MPLA. Between August 1987 and March 1988, Cuito Cuanavale saw widespread fighting, not only between Angolan forces, but also involving the South African Defence Force (SADF) and Cuban Revolutionary Armed Forces (FAR). It is often cited as a key turning point in the Angolan Civil War, and although historians on both sides still disagree as to who won the confrontation, it is clear that this battle led directly to the withdrawal of both Cuban and South African forces from the Angolan theatre.

My original journey to Cuito Cuanavale had not been easy. In 2012 the Angolan government had just completed a new airport in town, in order to shuttle in their dignitaries to inaugurate a museum celebrating the MPLA's glorious victory over the Apartheid South African invaders. However, there were no commercial flights landing here, so it was a long bus ride from Kuito for me. Once dropped off in the nearest large settlement of Menongue, I then took my life in my hands and hitched a lift on an old American school bus, which plied the pot-holed route down to Cuito Cuanavale. Despite the dangerous road conditions, the bus driver, who had spent much of his life in a refugee camp in neighbouring Zambia, was in an inexplicable rush and we rarely dipped below 100kmph. Lurching wildly from side to side to avoid pot holes, it was a miracle we did not flip over. Despite arriving in one of the most mine-affected areas of Angola, I felt much safer stepping off the bus at my final destination.

My guide during the visit was Edson, who ran the HALO Trust's work in the area. Smartly dressed and very sincere, he told me incredible tales of his time during the civil war and the ways in which local communities were still feeling the impacts over a decade on. Edson took great pride in the work that they were doing, helping local communities access new farmland and slowly reducing the ever-present threat of losing a limb (or worse) while travelling between villages.

Sadly, I did not have to look far to see people who had been injured by landmines and only a few days after I left the area a group of children were killed while playing with a live mortar round they had found in the bush.

The HALO Trust has done excellent work in demarcating the minefields themselves, so now it is much clearer to the local communities where is safe to walk and where is not. In their desperation for arable land, many people are working the soil right up to the landmine marker sticks, which indicate danger with a red-and-white painted tip. Others have been observed knowingly heading into the minefields to collect firewood, taking serious risks to meet their basic needs.

One of the first sites Edson took me to featured the shattered remains of an Angolan Armed Forces Toyota Land Cruiser, which had driven over a Cuban anti-tank mine. The Cubans had a nasty habit of stacking mines on top of each other, or burying further explosives with the mine to increase the impact. The distance the vehicle had flown, from the site of the initial detonation to its final resting place, gave an idea of the devastating power of the explosion. All of the occupants were killed. Another landmark in the minefields was a South African Olifant battle tank, which had been disabled after losing a caterpillar track in an explosion during the battle.

The process of removing mines from the ground safely is painstakingly slow and, despite all the precautionary measures in place, it remains a hazardous job for those undertaking it. Looking around the minefields in Cuito Cuanavale, I was struck by just how many mines there were, both in terms of variety and density. You did not need to be an expert to spot some of them, especially those that had been uncovered by rainfall and simply sat on the surface. There were mines with tripwires, pressure sensitive mines, mines designed to maim and those designed to kill, as well as numerous larger anti-tank mines.

Dealing with all of these threats in a safe and effective way takes patience and professionalism, which the HALO Trust workers had in abundance. I spent a few nights with them in their headquarters and was amazed at the austere conditions in which they were working (and the unforgiving weather). The criticism of many NGOs work-

Figure 8 – Edson and disabled South African tank (April 2012)

ing in areas such as this is that a lot of charitable donations get spent on fat expatriate salaries and new Toyota Land Cruisers. In fact, in 2014, the founder and former Chief Executive of the HALO Trust, Guy Willoughby, faced controversy when the *Sunday Telegraph* printed details of his compensation package. There could be no such accusations of extravagance in Cuito Cuanavale. I stayed in a bare concrete room with no electricity, with our one luxury being firing up the diesel generator to watch a football match on the TV in the evening!

There are years of mine clearance work left to do in Angola, and my 2012 visit helped me appreciate the scale of the problem, as well as what needs to be done to provide a solution. The world's largest landmine clearance agencies have set themselves an ambitious goal: a landmine-free world by 2025. This is not impossible. Mozambique was once one of the most mine-affected countries in the world, but after 22 years of work by the HALO Trust, in September 2015 it was declared mine-free. This means focusing on the remaining heavily mined countries of Angola, Afghanistan, Cambodia and Zimbabwe.

Having seen the impacts of landmines in Angola, Alfy and I both agreed that the HALO Trust was the right charity to support.

We woke up on Monday 6 June cold and unrefreshed. It was time to start hiking. Our mission for the next two days was straightforward: load our 105kg of gear onto the buggy and haul it about 50km along a sand track to Soma Kuanza, a nearby settlement where the Kwanza River becomes navigable (according to satellite photography).

The buggy we used had had an interesting life. I believe it was originally imported to Angola by a French oil worker who used it to kite-buggy on Angola's sand flats. I inherited the three-wheeled beast from a maths-teaching colleague called Marek at the international school. Between 2009 and 2012 the only use it got was being thrown in the back of our 4×4 on surf trips, for random spins down the hills that lead to the beaches south of Luanda. After a couple of high-speed crashes, we decided this was not a good use of our time: the buggy had no brakes, limited steering and we did not have helmets. For the next two years it sat gathering dust in my apartment.

When I left Luanda in June 2014 I gave it to Alfy. At the time, I had no idea what he planned on doing with it, but it is lucky that he kept it. In the run-up to the expedition he was able to find a welder who cut it up (to make it collapsible), improved the carrying capacity and added handles so that it could be dragged from the front. A little bit like my tent, the buggy could have done with some more testing before our trip began.

We had immediate issues with the buggy handles. Alfy preferred to drag with the handles behind his back. I preferred to drive with the handles in front of my hips. After only a few kilometres of painfully slow dragging and blistered hands, we had to improvise handle extensions. Then there was the carrying capacity. We could not fit our rucksacks on the buggy, so we had to wear those while dragging. It was apparent that this was not the most efficient use of the wheeled cart, so again we stopped and did some quick improvisation.

We extended the buggy's carrying capacity by adding a wooden frame to the back. Bags dropped off every now and then and the odd bit of kit dragged along the floor, but this was a much more comfortable setup, which allowed us to reach the blistering speed of 3kmph! We saw some Angolan women down by a stream washing their clothes in the late morning, but other than that we were alone all day.

Part way through the afternoon we reached a gentle, open escarpment between two wooded plateaus. Theoretically you could fit a 4×4 down this white sand track, but in reality the only markings were from footprints, and even those seemed to be very old. We stood at the top of the hill and looked out to the horizon. The fields were a dark orange with knee-high grass. The surrounding forest was thick, with the odd clear area caused by wildfires.

This would be a perfect spot to get some drone footage. I unpacked the DJI Phantom 3, went through all the pre-flight checks and launched it, giving us great views of the surrounding area from 100m altitude. Over on the horizon was Mumbwé village, the nearest settlement to the source, a couple of brown specks in our viewfinder. The clear blue sky was a striking contrast to the greens and yellows of the wooded grassland surrounding us. The bright orange earth of the hillsides also stood out. This was a very different landscape to the one I was used to around Luanda.

We used the drone to film a section of us walking. For some reason, after landing the drone it took off again, almost cutting Alfy's hands as he went to retrieve it. It then flew off towards the horizon, refusing to respond to my remote controller.

'Well, that was an extravagant use of £500,' Alfy deadpanned as I struggled to regain control of the drone.

'Yes, I have no idea where it's going! Maybe we should have done a little more flying practice back in Huambo?'

We both stood there, watching helplessly as our expensive investment floated away. Miraculously, after flying far enough away to be irretrievable, the drone changed its mind and calmly turned around, returned to where we were standing and landed (all without me touching the controls). Our faith in the drone technology was temporarily restored, but the whole episode had wasted precious hiking time.

By the time darkness fell we had covered 20km, a vaguely

Figure 9 – Drone footage of our hike (6 June 2016)

respectable figure for day one. We collapsed into our tents utterly exhausted but relieved that we were making good progress and that all of the equipment was working as expected – apart from the drone. And Alfy's sleeping bag. And the buggy. And my tent.

On Tuesday 7 June Alfy's alarm went off before sunrise. It had been another freezing cold night and there was ice on our tents. I am not a morning person at the best of times, but getting out of my sleeping bag and into my cold, filthy clothes in the pitch black was a real struggle. Before heading off we re-lit the fire to keep the insects at bay and cooked up some breakfast.

Food options were limited due to weight considerations. We had cereal bars for times when it was not practical to cook in the morning and porridge with dried fruit for when it was. We were both ravenous and wolfed down our 50g of dried porridge, mixed with a delicious treat that my girlfriend had given us before our departure: single-serving Nutella packets! At this early stage of the journey, the excitement of finally being out in the bush overwhelmed any sense of missing loved ones back home. However, as time went on, anxiety at separation from Steph and Marie-Louise respectively would be a feature of many of my riverside conversations with Alfy.

Once back on the trail the day was tough but uneventful. We

trekked about 15km, thankful for the shade the forest canopy provided. Apart from the weight, it was a pleasant way to spend the day.

'Whereabouts did you grow up then, Alfy?' I realised that despite knowing each other for almost four years, we had never really talked about our backgrounds. I just knew that Alfy had studied Anthropology at Cambridge University.

'We live on a farm out in Kent. I grew up round there, studied at Sevenoaks.'

I shook my head. 'Unbelievable! I went to school at Ardingly College. We used to play you guys at sports!' It turned out we had gone to secondary school within 30km of each other, and at exactly the same time, although the odds of us having faced each other in a sports team were quite slim. Alfy tended to be in the First XI for most sports, whereas the height of my athletic achievement was captaining the Fifth XI football team one season!

We chatted about our families, mutual acquaintances in Angola, summer travel plans, anything to take our minds off the long road ahead. Our trek took us past a number of artificial bee hives in the trees, placed there by local communities. They were long tubes constructed of bark and string, wedged into tall branches. Bees loved them, as they provided the perfect cover for building their nests. The honey from the bees in this part of Angola tastes smoky and less sweet than the honey you find in supermarkets. It is also believed to have medicinal qualities by local communities.

While we sat having lunch – a mixture of peanuts, biltong and anything else we had that did not need cooking – an Angolan couple appeared out of nowhere and said hello. We were surprised to see them, having been completely alone for over 24 hours. The man came and sat in the shade with us, looking over all of our equipment and taking a particular interest in the buggy.

'*O que é isso? Tem um motor?*'

He wanted to know if our Klepper had a motor. This was a question we were asked frequently on the trip. Just why people thought that two men would choose to paddle down the river with a motor hidden in their bags was a mystery.

'*Não não! Este é o nosso caiaque.*'

Alfy picked up a few struts and mimed putting them together, assembling the kayak. I paddled in the air, just to emphasise it ran on muscle power, not petrol.

The man shook his head.

'*Não, não pode ser…*'

He poked around in the bags, lifting out the canvas skin and the wooden ribs.

'*Está quebrado?*' (Is it broken?)

We certainly hoped not. The Klepper had only been dragged for two days. It was a bit early for it to break! A combination of the man's lack of Portuguese and the absurdity of our situation prevented us from getting the message across. The most prevalent language in this area was Mbwela and we did not know any useful phrases. Eventually we said our goodbyes, parted company and pushed on to Soma Kuanza.

We could hear Soma Kuanza long before we saw it. As darkness fell, *kizomba* music came blasting down from the area of high ground the town is perched on. The last 3km of our walk involved a progressively steeper sandy hill which sapped us of both energy and morale. By the time we rolled into town we were exhausted, mosquito-bitten and our hands were a blistered mess but the joy of having made it masked all the pain from the 30km of hiking that day.

Like many rural Angolan settlements, Soma Kuanza was a series of mud and tin shacks clustered around a few official buildings, in this case, the police station and the MPLA headquarters. In 1991, Soma Kuanza had been one of the 22 Areas of Assembly for demobilised UNITA troops agreed in the Bicesse Accords. The area had experienced a brief period of peace before the September 1992 general elections broke down and the two sides went back to war.

The people of Soma Kuanza were all gearing up for a heavy night on the Cuca (the delicious national beer) and shouted their welcomes to us as we rolled down the main strip. Our first move was to find a local shop with a generator and purchase some soft drinks. Alfy and I consumed six cans of Coca Cola between us before doing anything else. We craved sugar for the entire journey and getting it in refreshing liquid form after sweating all day and struggling with the water filtration devices felt amazing.

The local police welcomed us into their compound with open arms. The Chief of Police in Soma Kuanza, Comandante Teodoro Guilherme Gumbe, had been pre-notified of our arrival by the HALO Trust and was delighted to see us. He let us set up our tents in the courtyard of the police station and reassured us that we would face no *confusão* in the town under his watch.

> ### *Confusão*
> Ryszard Kapuściński, a Polish journalist who visited Luanda in 1974 on the eve of independence, defined this frequently used term well in his book, *Another Day of Life*:
>
> '*Confusão* is a good word, a synthesis word, an everything word. In Angola, it has its own specific sense and is literally untranslatable. To simplify things: *Confusão* means confusion, a mess, a state of anarchy and disorder. *Confusão* is a situation created by people, but in the course of creating it they lose control and direction, becoming victims of *confusão* themselves. There is a sort of fatalism in *confusão*.'
>
> My own experience was that *confusão* lives on in Angola even after the war. It would materialise in situations as diverse as road traffic accidents or in the queue for the bank. People were often keen to point out that someone was causing *confusão*, but this did not help to sort it out. My most frequent interaction with the phenomenon was on the football pitch, in our friendly Monday night kick-about. The Brazilian and Angolan players would hurl the term at each other frequently whenever there was claim of a foul. Sure enough, with no referee present to control the *confusão*, it would often spread. A couple of times we had to call half-time early. Hardly a serious inconvenience when compared to Kapuściński's experiences of it during the war.

We spent the evening cooking up spicy spaghetti with tuna that we bought in a local market and chatting to all the police officers.

Comandante Gumbe promised us that in the morning a police escort would show where we could get in the river and start kayaking. Everyone we spoke to also reassured us that there were no hippos in the area. One lieutenant pointed to his rifle:

'*Foram todos comidos durante a guerra.*'

The hippos around here were all eaten during the civil war. The conservationist in me was saddened. The kayaker in me was quietly relieved. Alfy and I headed out and managed to find an ice-cold Cuca in town.

Figure 10 – With our police hosts in Soma Kuanza (7 June 2016)

That evening, we sat around our gas cooker chatting to Comandante Gumbe's men about our expedition and how we hoped to raise money for landmine clearance. Comandante Gumbe reassured us that we were safe from *bandidos* (bandits) while under his care.

'Are there a lot of bandits around here?'

This was a risk we had not really investigated before starting.

'Oh, not now. But there used to be. Now they are all gone.'

Comandante Gumbe reflected soberly on his efforts to eradicate the bandits. Apparently there used to be a lot of bandits in these parts during the civil war.

Every one of the men around us had a story of loss from the times of the civil war. From a military historian's perspective, Angola is both a horrifying and fascinating place. From 1975 to 1991 it was the site of one of the largest and deadliest proxy conflicts of the Cold War. By the time the Angolan Civil War was over in 2002, 500,000 people had died, a third of the country's 13 million population was internally displaced and 450,000 were refugees in other countries. Soma Kuanza and its residents had seen some serious fighting.

The next day began with panic.

'Oscar, where's the GPS device?'

I could tell from the urgency of Alfy's voice that he was not messing around.

'I don't know. You were in charge of that! You had it in your hand last night, I remember. The yellow one?'

Alfy had last checked it the night before and we had both seen it before going to bed. It was a bright-yellow Garmin and difficult to miss. Comandante Gumbe enlisted all of his men to help us track it down, and soon their parade ground was strewn with our equipment as we tore everything apart to find it. Although we did have a backup GPS device, the other one did not have all of our waypoints plotted onto it and it would be a huge risk starting the expedition with only one device. An hour into our frantic hunt, Alfy reached into the front pocket of his rucksack and pulled out the yellow device.

'Oscar, I found it. What should we say?'

He looked suitably sheepish. Despite the meticulous attention to detail in his planning for this trip, I would soon find that Alfy had a knack for temporarily losing bits of expedition kit.

'I guess we just say we found it and apologise. Hey, at least we didn't accuse anyone of stealing it.'

The police were kind enough not to call us idiots, but I am sure that is what they were thinking.

The entry point to the Kwanza River was a few kilometres back down the hill we had hiked up to get into town the night before. Our departure was quite the event in town, and we were given an armed escort of no fewer than four police officers. There was some back-

and-forth discussion from the more senior police officers as to where exactly to drop us off, but eventually we found the spot that they said marked the beginning of the navigable Kwanza River. It was a narrow section of river, no wider than 5m, with a small wooden footbridge built across it. The water was crystal clear, around 3m in depth with long green aquatic plants swaying in the leisurely current.

My first thought was 'that looks good enough to drink'. My second was 'that looks deep enough for a crocodile to hide in'.

The police escort were still very sceptical about our claims that the dusty bags we were dragging behind us contained a large water craft. As Alfy laid out the skin and then began assembling the wooden skeleton frame, they became increasingly impressed. As did I. Beyond seeing her partially assembled in Alfy's living room a week prior, this was the first time I had seen the Klepper fully constructed and ready to go. I was amazed at the speed with which Alfy was able to get her put together. It cannot have been more than 20 minutes from first stopping by the side of the river to having all our gear loaded onto the kayak, ready to get started. We waved goodbye to the police, hoisted the Angolan flag on the back of the Klepper and set off.

The first kilometre or so was easy. The current was fast enough that the only paddling we needed to do was for steering. The river was still very narrow at this point, and at over 5.4m long the Klepper kept threatening to wedge into the bends. Alfy, being the taller and stronger paddler, was sat in the back controlling the rudder with his foot pedals. I was in the front, mainly pushing us off the banks using my paddle. Even with all the curves, this was a lot easier than the previous two days of hiking and being down near the cool water level was a pleasant change. We glided along without a care in the world for the next half an hour.

Then we hit the reeds. The narrow water channel opened out into a broad marsh, with no clear waterway, and the flow rate dropped. Perhaps we had taken a wrong turn, or perhaps the residents of Soma Kuanza had a different definition of 'navigable' than we did.

'Alfy, I thought you said you'd mapped this section out? How can this look navigable from satellite photography?'

'I did, I did. Hopefully it will open out soon. We just need to keep pressing forwards.'

Alfy was very single-minded in this regard, stubborn even. We were in for a long day.

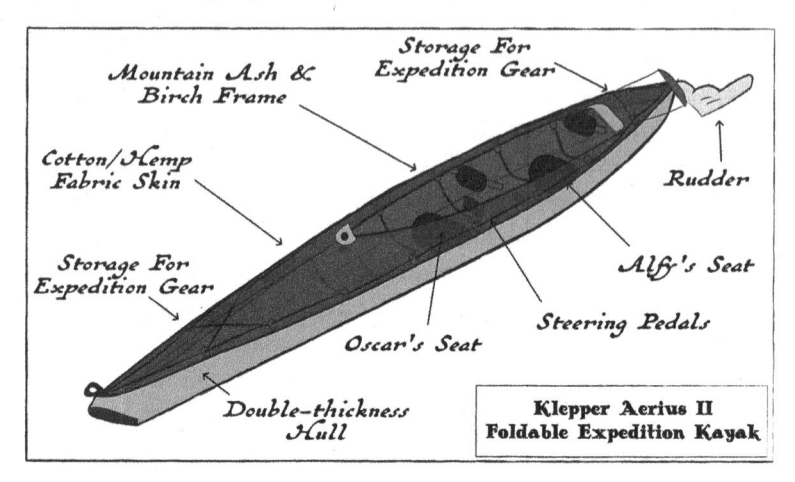

Figure 11 – Klepper Aerius II diagram. Image credit: Michael Peters

For the next eight hours we hacked away at the reeds using a machete, pulling ourselves through such narrow channels that it was almost impossible to use the paddles. One of us would work the rudder and the other would kneel on the front of the Klepper, punting along or physically pulling us forwards using the undergrowth for leverage. A couple of times we dragged the kayak out of the water only to re-enter in an oxbow lake. Often the water was completely still, giving no clue as to which direction the flow was heading. The sharp water grasses sliced up our forearms and the insects had a field day.

'Alfy, we're lost.'

'No, we'll be fine. We just need to keep heading that way.' He pointed his paddle into the reeds, at nothing in particular.

'Let's launch the drone. See if we can get an aerial view of where we are going.'

'That'll take ages. We don't have time for that. We just need to press on.'

It was amazing how quickly we had become lost and how difficult the expedition was already turning out to be. I began to doubt Alfy's planning. What on earth were we doing in this bog?

A few hours into the ordeal we heard two fishermen talking in the distance. We had no way of working out how far away they were or of getting to them. Their voices faded into the distance well before we could ask for help.

Disheartened and utterly exhausted, it was threatening to get dark and we could see no suitable location to put the Klepper ashore and camp. We ended up mooring her to some reeds and having to hack our way to the bank in order to unload. Stepping out of the kayak, we sank knee deep into the bog, soaking our boots. That night we camped in a mosquito-infested swamp, the jubilation of that morning all but forgotten. It was amazing how quickly our fortunes had changed.

On Thursday, 9 June we set off early, determined to escape the marsh and get some mileage under our belts. We needed to complete at least 50km per day while out on the water in order to have any hope of finishing on time, so we were technically already behind by the fourth day!

'Alfy, this is a disaster. We can't spend any more time hacking at these reeds. We're moving at a snail's pace.'

'I know, I know. But it has to open up soon. None of this was on the satellite photography. It has to start flowing soon.'

I did not share Alfy's optimism. I thought of the Sudd in South Sudan, that vast swamp on the River Nile, which stretches over 200km. How far had we come through this Kwanza swamp? Perhaps 10km?

After a few more hours of hacking at reeds, we heard the rush of flowing water. I could see ripples forming in the dense reeds in front of us. Alfy was the first to see the opening, as he was sat in the front of the Klepper.

'Boom! I told you it would open up!'

The flow rate sped up and we were swept out into open water again, which was a relief and validation of Alfy's route planning. With clear passage ahead of us, we were able to settle into a routine and smash through 25km before lunch.

An hour after lunch, I began to feel a twinge in my lower back. Assuming it was just fatigue, I thought nothing of it and kept paddling; we were making great progress and needed to make up for the slow start the day before. Over the course of the next 10km, the pain began radiating up my spine and around my waist. It quickly escalated to the point that I was doubled over, no longer able to paddle.

'Something's really wrong. My back is completely shot.'

'OK, well, just do what you can. I'll keep paddling, don't worry.' Alfy seemed remarkably calm given the difficult situation.

For the last hour of daylight, I was able to make minimal contributions to the paddling while Alfy picked up the slack, having to work twice as hard to keep us moving forwards. Alfy stayed positive, trying to suggest solutions: we tried a different paddling style and pace, as well as shifting me in my seat. But nothing made any difference.

I sat in front of him feeling utterly dejected. What was wrong? Had I not done enough training? How were we ever going to finish if this was the result after half a day of proper exertion on the water? Alfy tried to be as supportive as possible, telling me we would find a solution once we camped for the night. But in the meantime I had to sit there listening to him struggle to carry my dead weight, unable to help in any way.

That evening was very difficult. We actually found a good camping spot, with easy river access and a ledge to pull the Klepper out of the water for the night. We were on a foggy, rocky hilltop, with a lone tree and an angry crow for company. We could see the remains of an old fire, which we quickly re-lit, presumably left behind by a previous fishing expedition. There was also a great area of flat bank sheltered by trees, making putting up the tents quite straightforward. Wishing to avoid the difficult conversation, we sat watching the roaring fire, eating our expedition rations in silence. Eventually, I said what we were both thinking.

'I don't think I can manage 50km of paddling every day.'

Alfy was calm, but also brutally pragmatic.

'You have to. To slow down now would essentially be to concede that we are not going to finish.'

He was right, frustrating as that was. I felt the anger well up inside me, but had nowhere to direct it. Was it fair to be angry at Alfy? Probably not. But I was exhausted and not thinking logically.

We sat together and mapped out the route in front of us. At least 1,000km more paddling to be done before Monday 11 July – the date that Alfy had to be back in Luanda for work. The reality of our situation came as a crushing blow. Unless we found a solution, I would need to go through that day's pain at least 20 more times to finish on time.

This was Alfy's fault for planning an overly ambitious daily distance target. Why could we not do the trip more slowly, say 40km per day? Why had he not found more accurate flow rate data for the river? I did not ask any of these questions out loud. Alfy could just as easily have asked why I had not trained harder for the expedition. After all, he was finding it pretty easy going so far, until he had to paddle without my help.

I went to bed utterly dejected. Why had I not done more training? Why had I not been more closely involved in the route planning? I had read numerous accounts of the extreme highs and lows of remote expedition travel, but I did not expect to be facing this type of low so early in the journey. Sleep came quickly and my dreams were filled with images of failure.

On Friday, 10 June we were once again up before dawn, but it took a good three hours for us to set off. Alfy tended to react a lot more quickly to our alarm, but then also took longer to get ready. On this occasion, I was in no hurry to jump back in the kayak, afraid that I would be plagued by the same back pain as the day before. Alfy revealed that he had been bitterly cold that night in his two-season sleeping bag.

'Wait until the gear reviews at the end of this trip!'

We both laughed, but this was little consolation.

Visibility was very poor at 20m because of the morning fog. We slipped cautiously back onto the water, wary that the river was now wide and deep enough for hippos. Our first three hours of kayaking were uneventful. My back was miraculously fine and eventually we warmed up when the sun burned away the fog. The layers of clothes came off and the sunscreen went on.

The dull splash of the paddles entering the water was hypnotic. At 11am we were snapped out of our trance by the sound of heavy plant machinery up ahead in the distance. Rounding a corner, we saw a Chinese-made bulldozer and then an excavator trundling along a ridgeline. They were busy pushing material into the river to create a crossing.

As we floated up to this inconvenient obstacle, one of the digger drivers did a double-take, then hopped out of his cab to say hello. Nelo was a big jovial lad from a settlement 30km away. He was sporting a brown t-shirt with his own name emblazoned across the front. We shouted our greetings to him and waved our paddles.

'Welcome!' He motioned for us to moor by the crossing, and we got out and shook hands.

'What are you doing here? Where have you come from?'

'Soma Kuanza, the source of the Kwanza River, back there...' Alfy pointed over his shoulder.

'Ehhhh!' Nelo exclaimed, in classic Angolan fashion. Obviously impressed by our claim, he whistled loudly and a friend appeared from behind another excavator in the distance.

'Hey, Indio, come and meet these guys. They are kayaking the whole river!'

Indio skulked over, his thin frame and sunken eyes regarding us suspiciously.

'The whole river? Aren't you afraid of the hippos? Or the crocodiles? You're crazy.'

After reassuring them that we knew what we were doing, Nelo laughed and told us that he was working on creating an access road for an Angolan diamond concession that had just started up nearby.

Angola is one of the world's seven largest rough diamond-producing countries, and although most of her diamonds are mined up in the north-east of the country, we knew that the Kwanza River was also a rich source. It was surprising to see this level of exploration activity in such a remote location, especially so early in the trip. We were also pleasantly surprised by the welcome we were receiving from our first mine workers.

Many of the warnings back in Luanda had been to stay away from any diamond activities, as the miners tend to be armed and are often carrying out the work illegally, not keen to be seen by outsiders. Endiama E.P., the national diamond company of Angola, is the sole concessionaire for diamond mining rights, but their regulatory abilities did not appear to stretch this far into the bush. We were expecting a few artisanal miners, known as *garimpeiros*, but not an industrial-scale operation like this.

Had our expedition been taking place 15 years earlier, we would have been firmly in UNITA territory here. The MPLA financed their civil war effort through oil sales. UNITA did the same by exploiting inland Angola's abundant diamond resources, such as the ones we were now kayaking over. Global Witness estimated that UNITA obtained revenues of $3.72 billion between 1992 and 1998 from diamond sales alone. Controversy surrounding UNITA's diamond sales and their role in prolonging the conflict led to the adoption of the Kimberley Process in 2003, a diamond certification scheme to prevent conflict diamonds, or blood diamonds, from entering the global rough diamond market.

Figure 12 – Illegally mined diamonds, Lunda Norte, Angola (April 2012)

Nelo and his friends showed us a route to carry the kayak around the obstacle and reassured us that there were no hippos in the area, although there were some a little further along. Even when emptied out the Klepper weighed 45kg, making it no fun at all to carry over uneven ground on your shoulders. It was a relief to throw it back into the water and load up. Nelo insisted that we swap numbers before we headed off and told us to call if we needed any help.

'Is there any phone signal down here?' Alfy asked, looking at the zero bars on his phone screen.

'Oh no,' laughed Nelo. 'Not for miles! Good luck!'

After a few more hours of paddling, my crippling back pain returned. There seemed to be no logic to it: we were doing exactly the same thing that we had been doing for the previous five hours. In a depressingly familiar pattern, my pauses became more and more frequent until at the 55km mark I stopped completely.

'Listen, I don't think I can hack paddling on my own right now, I'm exhausted. Let's set up camp around here and come up with a plan for tomorrow,' Alfy said.

Again, he was pretty upbeat about this serious threat to our expedition.

I could hardly stand to lift myself out of the kayak and set up the camp. We chose another former fisherman's camp, complete with wood to burn and a flat spot for the kayak. I was eager to rest my back and sat down into my folding aluminium camp stool, only to have one of the legs immediately snap. This was the only chair I had and now it was gone, broken in the first week of the expedition. Our kit selection was turning into a comedy of errors.

Alfy and I had a similar conversation to the night before about my back. I was at a loss as to what to do. He later revealed to me that he too was very concerned at this stage, as despite his offer to paddle for me, he would have struggled to complete 1,000km of kayaking with a partner who only paddled for 60 per cent of each day. Having so publicly committed to completing this journey, I was now facing the very real prospect of failure: either through having to pull out from injury, or through slowing the expedition down to the point that Alfy had to leave before completion on 11 July. Alfy ended the evening with this comment:

'We have to try something different. Maybe it's your seating position? It doesn't matter how long it takes tomorrow morning, you have to adjust the kayak until you are comfortable for 60km. It's worth making the time investment now.'

The next morning (Saturday, 11 June), we were up early again.

'Bloody hell, my tent is freezing! Why the hell did I only bring a two-season sleeping bag?'

Alfy had had another difficult night with the temperatures and exited from his tent wearing almost every piece of clothing he had brought. We both laughed again. It was a great moment of levity in an otherwise tense start to the day. I was also continuing to have issues with my tent and woke up with wet feet.

As we both stood round preparing to leave, I captured one of my best photos of the entire journey: Alfy in the fog, in front of the ice-covered Klepper. At least our suffering looked picturesque.

Figure 13 – Alfy suffering in the morning cold (11 June 2017)

Before setting out we wedged one of the spare buggy tyres under my seat in the Klepper, which raised me up about four inches off the base of the kayak. We also reorganised the load space within the hollow kayak to ensure that I had room to stretch my legs out.

A few hours into our paddling, Alfy looked at his GPS, amazed. 'That's 25km already! How's the back feeling?'

'Completely fine. I could do this all day!'

What an incredible difference this small adjustment made. That was the last of my back pain for the remainder of the trip: it had nothing to do with a lack of preparation and everything to do with my incorrect angle of attack on the water. Alfy and I were both seriously relieved as we glided along the river that morning, chatting away happily, things finally going as we had expected.

In order to be as efficient as possible, our lunch breaks did not involve getting out of the kayak, but simply allowing it to drift while eating in our seats. Alfy would occasionally have to engage the rudder to point us around a corner. We even came up with a system whereby one of us leaned precariously over the side to urinate, while the other counterbalanced.

This was a pretty typical approach that we used most days. During our 30- to 45-minute lunchbreak, we could drift up to 2km if the current was going fast, a great trick to stay on schedule. The only issue with this approach was that it meant we were gliding through the water silently, hardly disturbing the surface.

Before setting out on the expedition, Alfy and I did a lot of research on the risks we would face while out on the river. Hippos and crocodiles kept coming up. Alfy spoke to conservationist Dr Steve Boyes and two of his team members, who had led a number of river expeditions for National Geographic through southern Angola as part of the Okavango Wilderness Project. He also spoke to Lorenzo Amaral, a Portuguese national who grew up exploring the Angolan bush, as well as his housemate Joost, who had experience as a South African safari guide. We even tried contacting the Portuguese Hydrographic Society to see if they had mapped the dangers on the river. It turns out they had not. The general consensus seemed to be that crocodiles would not be an issue as long as we kept our bodies out of the water, whereas hippos might cause problems.

Angola is home to all sorts of crocodile species, including the potentially dangerous Nile crocodile (*Crocodylus niloticus*). It was this species that pulled renowned South African outdoorsman Hendrik Coetzee out of his kayak and killed him on the Congo River in December 2010. Closer to home, political activist Isaías Cassule was murdered by Angolan security forces in May 2012 and, it was later revealed, his body fed to crocodiles in the Bengo River. Between January and May 2016, just before we arrived in Angola for our expedition, at least eight Angolans were killed in crocodile attacks on the banks of the Cunene River, in the municipality of Matala, southern Huíla province. Despite these horror stories, the experts agreed that it was very rare for crocodiles to attack people in a boat, especially one as large as 5.4m. They are ambush predators and far more likely to attack people (especially small children) collecting water on the river bank.

On the hippo side, the stories were more concerning. Anecdotal evidence suggests that hippos are one of the most dangerous land animals in Africa, responsible for thousands of deaths per year. Dr Boyes' expedition had even been attacked by hippos while in the Angolan highlands on the Cuito River in 2015, with an aggressive male piercing their dugout canoe with his incisors and throwing the occupants into the river. Luckily nobody was seriously hurt.

Hippos are surprisingly agile in water, able to swim faster than we could ever paddle, and can sprint up to 30kmph over short distances on land. Males weigh up to four and a half tonnes and do not take kindly to intruders in their patch of the river. They spend a lot of their time underwater during the day to avoid the heat, resurfacing to breathe every three to five minutes. They come out of the river at night to graze.

We had briefly looked into getting a rifle for the expedition, but had been told that this would be useless against hippos: their 5cm-thick skin renders them virtually bullet proof to conventional ammunition and we would have little hope of shooting one before it upturned our boat. Under these circumstances, avoidance was definitely the best approach.

How to avoid hippo attacks is the subject of some controversy, but Alfy and I managed to piece together some rough guidelines from the expert advice we received: do not surprise them, make sure they know where you are at all times, avoid their offspring and always give them a clear path to escape you. By our third day of kayaking, there were signs of hippo activity all along the river: we could see their footprints in the mud of the riverbanks and they had trampled out wide pathways through the reeds to get into and out of the water. But as yet, we had not actually seen a hippo. On Saturday lunchtime, as we sat drifting along eating our biltong, all this changed.

We passed a lone fisherman in his dugout canoe and asked him if he had seen any hippos. He told us that he had and that there were some around just up ahead. We thanked him for the warning, put our food away and got our paddles out again. No sooner had we splashed the surface of the water for the first time than we heard a loud noise behind Alfy.

It sounded like a burst tyre deflating rapidly. Being at the front of the kayak, I could not see the cause of the sound as it was obscured by Alfy's torso. But I did not need to see. We both knew what it was: we had just drifted directly over a hippo and it had surfaced behind our rear rudder.

'Oh crap! Go, go, go, paddle!' Alfy screamed.

We dug in as hard and as fast as possible to move away from danger. Over the next 15 seconds I waited to feel the hit under the boat as the hippo jaws struck us. The Klepper skin was thin rubber on the bottom. When Dr Boyes' expedition was attacked, the hippo rammed its tusk through two inches of solid *makoro* wood. Our Klepper skin did not stand a chance.

But the hit never came. We foolishly raced around a tight corner on the inside edge, cutting close to the reeds to get away faster. There was a crash from up in the reeds and then an almighty splash right under the front of our kayak. The plant growth had obscured our view, but another hippo, startled by our sudden appearance around the corner, had rushed down the bank towards the safety of the deep water, missing the front of the Klepper by less than a metre. We sprinted for another 200m before even thinking of looking behind us. The adrenaline had us both shaking. Our first encounter with the Kwanza's hippos had been far too close for comfort.

Looking back, we could see the hippos for the first time, floating in the middle of the river. They were flapping their brown ears (tiny little ears in comparison to their bath tub-sized bodies) and flexing their large nostrils in displeasure at our rude disturbance. Despite being such large animals, you see little of them while they are in the water. If they are really trying to hide, only the contours of their nostrils and their bulging eyes sit just above the surface. They can only really be distinguished from a log or piece of debris by the fact that they remain steady in the water, creating a wave of turbulence behind them as the river flows past.

Determined to learn from our mistakes, we came up with a new strategy. Firstly, we made more noise as we were paddling along. Every 30 seconds or so, one of us would shout 'Hello, hippos!' at the top of our lungs. That should help them realise we were coming, even if the hippos did not speak English.

We also looked very closely at each side of the river bank for signs of hippo activity and carefully chose a side when going around a corner based on which one we thought was less likely to have hippos on it. Generally speaking, this meant going for the corner with better visibility and less foliage for hippos to hide in. On corners with reeds on both sides, we cautiously moved down the middle of the river. The hippos' instinct appeared to be to make a mad dash for the river's deepest point once we arrived, so we did not want to get in their way by appearing too fast or around a blind corner.

It did not take long before we saw more hippos. In fact, we heard the next group of three well before we saw them. Hippos trumpet, a deep booming noise somewhere between a pig snort and the beginning of a cow's moo. Their intonation and repetition makes it sound a little like they are laughing. This is disconcerting at first, especially when it rings out at night, but useful for getting a lock on their relative location. Eventually we rounded a corner and were confronted with the source of all the noise: three large hippos foraging in the reeds. They were partially submerged in the boggy reeds, massive bodies on full display, occasionally opening their jaws as if to yawn.

We stopped the kayak and faced them, with about 100m between us. We shouted hello, then began slapping the water with our paddles, to ensure that any other hippos under the surface had a good idea of where we were. The hippos reacted immediately, jumping straight into the deeper water, causing large bow waves, and vanishing to the centre of the river. After a few minutes, they popped up on the other side, revealing their locations with a deep exhalation of breath. They had moved underwater with impressive speed and were now looking straight at us.

In many ways, this was far more frightening than the previous encounter. There, we had acted purely on instinct and it had all been over before we had any time to really think about it. Now we were confronted with three dangerous wild animals that we were going to have to paddle towards to get past. Getting out and walking was simply not an option and anyway, the banks were a reed-filled mess. We were committed to paddling through this section.

'OK, I reckon we creep up the right-hand side until we are level with them. Then we sprint. What do you think, Oscar?'

I thought it was a terrible idea, but we had little choice. We were giving them as wide a berth as possible and there was no way they had not spotted us. These bulky giants sat in the water, perfectly still, unblinking eyes honed on us. Hopefully they would leave us alone, but if they wanted to attack, we were a very easy target.

Very slowly, in utter silence, we moved to the right-hand side of the river, trying to put as much distance between us and the hippos as possible. At the same time, we were wary of getting too close to the reeds, as our previous experience had shown us that these gargantuan creatures had no problems remaining invisible in only a small amount of foliage. All the while, the hippos looked at us, occasionally flapping their ears to keep insects away.

After 75m of paddling we were about level with them. They were now over on the other bank, perhaps 25m away, but seemed to be more interested in slowly heading upstream than chasing us. As soon as we were level we made a break for it, sprinting as fast as possible to put some distance between us. They reacted briefly as our paddles started kicking up more water, but then went back to their calm swim. We had made it.

After this sighting we were much more cautious as we paddled along. We were navigating along a relatively clear river at this point, never wider than 25m. Here the Kwanza cuts through a vast, flat, featureless expanse of reeds. Stood up on the occasional piece of solid bank, you could see all the way to the hills on the horizon in every direction. Down at water level, all you could see was clear blue sky, murky water and a wall of reeds on either side, often trampled from hippo activity. It was like a vast natural maze. Later that afternoon we reached another obstacle, which was a welcome break in the tense paddling.

Someone had stuck a series of 23 wooden poles into the river bed at regular intervals, strapping them together with twine and horizontal pieces of wood. It looked like a makeshift crossing point. To reinforce the structure, a number of thicker stakes with Y-sections cut into their heads had been jammed on the downstream side at a 45 degree angle, supporting it against the current. Silt and reeds had built up against the poles, creating a makeshift dam that meant the water level on one side was around 30cm higher than on the other.

We wasted a good hour trying to wedge the kayak through a gap in the dam before we conceded defeat and portaged around it. This was a slow process of unloading all our gear, carrying that around, then hauling the kayak up the bank and dragging it along the grass until it could re-enter the river on the other side of the obstacle.

On both sides of the dam there were signs of human activity: remnants of whittling, cut sections of net and even a few hand-made wooden fish traps. Alfy and I were unsure exactly what this structure was for, but given the paths leading up to it on both sides of the river, it made sense to assume it was a crossing point. These structures would be a regular obstacle for as long as the river was narrow and shallow.

Just before sunset, we entered an area we dubbed 'hippo alley'. The river narrowed, the reeds thickened and we could find no solid ground to land and camp for the night. All around us we could hear the hippos grunting and splashing around, although we could not see them directly. It was terrifying. Often we could not even see solid ground to swim towards if we were upturned, but we had to push on, hoping to find a more suitable camping spot further down the river.

Ten minutes turned into 30, and before we knew it the light was threatening to run out. Paddling this area in the dark was a terrible idea. Not only could we no longer see obstacles, but getting wet at this stage would have been dangerous given the way the temperature plummeted at night. Eventually, despite all the hippo noise, we found a dyke that had been dug into the side of the river, with the removed earth forming a nice elevated mound. It was as though someone had made us a private harbour. As with the earlier dam, we were fascinated and confused by these signs of human activity, but did not ask too many questions as we unloaded all the gear and hauled up the kayak.

The knee-high grass stretched for hundreds of metres and was trampled all around the area where we were stopping. We hoped that this was humans drying their fish rather than hippos grazing. As we lit our fire, we could hear some people on the other side of the river singing and rattling pans. We could not see them due to the long grass on that side, but it was reassuring to know we were not alone. As well as the humans, we heard a number of hippos that evening. They chimed in at around 6.30pm and would not shut up all night. Some of the grunts were very deep and very close. The fire kept them away and we fell asleep quickly, to the sounds of a whole village singing.

The next day we woke up and scraped the frost off our bags and tents. My first aim after exiting the warm cocoon of my tent was to get a fire lit and then pack up the kit explosion that inevitably occurred every evening. Despite our best intentions, the exhaustion of the day's paddling combined with our desperation to cook dinner usually resulted in a very messy campsite as we rushed to unpack essential gear before it got dark. It was a glorious sunny day but the tension was high as we headed back out onto a stretch of water we could hear was infested with hippos.

Rounding one corner that morning we bumped into a fisherman, slowly punting his way through the shallow reeds. Although it was illogical, any fear I felt on the river melted away as soon as we saw another human being. Talking with these fishermen also put our problems in perspective. João spent his days punting up and down the river, often camping in the bush during his fishing expeditions. He was in his early twenties, wearing three-quarter length khaki shorts and a green t-shirt with a faded sun on it and the name of a US middle school. His canoe was decrepit: it had numerous holes in the side, plugged with what looked like sods of earth. The edges were all chipped and only sat about an inch above the waterline. It wobbled precariously as he pushed himself along.

Beyond a coat and a cigarette lighter, João had none of the equipment required for such a cold night-time environment. By relying on a pole for propulsion, he was also committing himself to skirting the reeds, which often put him dangerously close to the hippos. We asked if he was afraid.

'*Sim, eles matam!*' (Yes, they kill!)

Being slow, unstable and impossible to propel through deep water, he was a sitting duck for a hippo attack. João calmly told us that he had been knocked out of his boat on a number of occasions, but never injured. We shuddered at the thought. He ended with a quote that was amusing in its chilling understatement:

'*Eles não respeitam o barco!*' (They do not respect the boat!)

Our questions to the fishermen we came across were invariably the same: where have you come from today? Are there hippos around here? Are there rapids or waterfalls further up? Where is the nearest village?

João was friendly and willing to help, as was every other fisherman we met. He laughed at our story of where we had come from and where we were trying to reach. He even sold us two fish for two hundred kwanzas. He tried to throw in a third free of charge, but we declined his kind offer, as we only required two for dinner and his total catch was not very large.

Our encounter with João and other fishermen taught us something about the way information travelled through this remote landscape. The fishermen had a limited range in their dugout canoes, with most having travelled less than 30km from their village either upstream or downstream. When discussing this area, 'the near river', they were experts: they could name landmarks, river features and exit points with precision. However, at the edges of their experience, they were more reliant on stories from other fishermen around the campfire or relatives who had travelled to other parts either on foot or using a bush taxi (usually a motorbike). It was here that the accuracy began to fade. We would often hear tales of waterfalls the size of mountains, huge pods of killer hippos or terrible rapids that could not be traversed. Thus, a vague question such as 'is there a waterfall up ahead?' would elicit a very different answer to 'have you navigated past a waterfall on your way here today?' Alfy and I quickly learned that only specific questions got reliable answers.

That afternoon at 2pm we saw two hippos. Using our pause-assess-creep-sprint technique, we managed to get past them without incident. At 3.15pm we had some more excitement when we disturbed a massive 3m crocodile sunning itself on the opposite river bank. This was the first and only time we saw a whole crocodile out of the water, and he was not happy, immediately launching himself into the depths and vanishing from sight.

We knew there were crocs this big in the Kwanza, as while living in Angola my friends and I had seen them on the golf course just south of Luanda. The owners of the course had built it near the River Kwanza in order to make irrigation easier. What they had not counted on was that their perfectly manicured putting greens would become a popular sunbathing hangout for all of the river's nearby crocodiles. It was advisable to take a drop shot rather than head into the water hazards to retrieve a golf ball on that course!

Other than our wildlife encounters, it was an uneventful day and we chose to stop in an empty fisherman's camp, complete with small thatch huts and a still smoking fire. The fishermen had done a great job of clearing the area of grass and there were even some banana trees being cultivated in a small field just behind the camp. A small path led off into the wilderness but we did not follow it. As with meeting the fisherman, it all served to make us feel less alone.

We laid all of our wet gear out on the thatch roof to dry in the last rays of the setting sun. Alfy put the fish in silver foil and lit a fire to cook them on. We were both very excited to be eating something that was not dehydrated beans with rice.

'Yeah, I'm not sure how this is going to turn out. Marie-Louise usually does most of the cooking in our house!'

We both reminisced fondly about the feast she had served us at

Alfy's flat the night before we set out for Huambo. Potatoes, steamed veg, meat that fell off the bone. There was even dessert. We would have given anything for a plate of her cooking that evening. Even at this early stage of our expedition, the rations were becoming monotonous and we were always going to bed hungry.

As it turned out, the fish were a bit of a disappointment: all bone and no meat, plus they mainly tasted of mud. It was still good to get some variation in our diet, and for two hundred kwanzas (officially $1.20, unofficially $0.33) we could hardly complain.

Full of weird muddy fish, we discussed the trip in front of our campfire.

'So how does this compare to your expectations so far?' I asked Alfy, keen to hear if this was as surreal for him as it was for me.

'Yeah, this is not how I was expecting it to be. Much more isolated. I thought there would be more communities by the side of the river and I definitely didn't expect this many hippos. I thought they had all been poached.'

As with the night before, we spent a short while chatting in front of the camp fire once it went dark, then passed out from exhaustion to the sounds of hippos grunting in the reeds nearby.

Figure 14 – Huts left by fishermen (12 June 2016)

On Monday, 13 June we were up early but could not leave due to fog affecting visibility. This gave us time to cook up some oats for breakfast, which was a rare treat. It also made Alfy feel a bit better about his tent leaking. His roof was leaking in a number of spots, dripping water down onto his head and torso throughout the night.

By the time we set off, a couple of fishermen had actually appeared from around the corner, which was great news after all the hippo calls the night before. This day set a new record for hippo sightings, with us spotting at least ten and hearing a lot more in the undergrowth. There were a few near misses, with hippos jumping into the river very close to us, to the point where their bow waves rocked our kayak violently.

In between the high-stress periods of dodging hippos, we began spotting some odd signs of human activity along the waterside. The first things we noticed were the same patches of digging that we had used as a harbour on Saturday evening. People had gone to a lot of trouble to dig channels from the river, about 1m wide, running into the surrounding fields. They only stretched about 2 or 3m, making them unsuitable for irrigation. Also, none of the land was cultivated, which was confusing.

As well as these channels, we frequently saw raggedy wooden poles, sticking out of the waterline like the beginning of a footbridge, but only ever stretching a little way out from the bank. Many of these seemed to have been deliberately covered in grass.

Alfy suggested that these might be a way of harnessing the wind on the river to dry thatch for roofing. Whatever they were, they had been left in a state of disrepair and were no longer being used by their original architects. It looked as though a great tidal wave had swept down the river, destroying everything in its path. We navigated around these obstacles carefully, wary of puncturing the skin of the Klepper on sharp underwater poles.

That evening, after a successful day of kayaking, we made camp on top of a wooded hill overlooking the river. By this stage, we were experts at judging the approach of darkness, and it was a boost to morale to have finished our allocation of kayaking and be able to set up camp with at least an hour of daylight left. This meant we could hang up clothes to dry and made pitching camp much quicker.

We ran around our new camp excitedly, unsure what to do with this precious hour of leisure time. Alfy and I both agreed that this was our best campsite to date: safely away from the water on high ground, sheltered by trees with fewer mosquitos, flat ground for camping and plenty of wood to burn. There was none of the usual hacking away with a machete to make space for the tents. We simply chucked them down under the biggest tree and lit a roaring fire.

That night, as we sat wolfing down our dinner of dehydrated Bolognese, we heard drumming coming from out on the plain. Soon, we could see the first licks of a large fire, about 2km in the distance. The flat, waterlogged landscape in front of us carried the sound well and we could almost hear the individual lyrics as a group of people started chanting in time with the drumming.

We could see the flames shooting up into the sky from our perch on the hill, so whoever it was had gone to a lot of trouble to gather that much fuel. They kept it burning for hours. We guessed it must have been a special occasion, or perhaps even a hippo hunt. As we went to sleep, we noted another added bonus of our location: the weather was much warmer than the previous nights.

Tuesday 14 June was our last planned heavy paddling session before a more relaxed push on Wednesday to the first key landmark in our journey: Kuito Bridge, the finish line for section one of the expedition.

Throughout the day we saw another puzzling feature as we paddled along: constant bush fires. The first thing we would notice would be the ash floating down into the river like grey snow. We would sometimes hear the fire well before we saw it, an alarming crackling sound that turned into a roar loud enough that we had to shout over it once we were close.

The plumes of smoke rose in great columns, stretching over vast swathes of the riverside scrubland. Were these natural features or was someone lighting them deliberately? The latter seemed more probable, given their high concentration across this one stretch of the Kwanza, although we never saw any people or evidence of the burned land being put to productive use. We pushed through these sections as fast as possible, to avoid inhaling the smoke, but also because the fires led to an exodus of large insects fleeing across the river and we were not keen on being swarmed.

We had smashed out 55km by 4pm and seen not one hippo, which was a welcome relief. Perhaps the drummer from the night before had scared them all away. Or perhaps it was all the fires. We did not really care, as long as they were not threatening our kayak. Once again, we were blessed with an excellent campsite, in a grassy field behind a row of large trees. A hundred metres further back from the river on our side was some woodland. On the other side of the bank was a cultivated field, with neat rows of tilled earth spread out over the size of a football pitch.

Sleep came quickly and we were both very excited about the following day. We only had 25km before we hit the Kuito Bridge, which marked the first third of our journey complete. The most remote section of the trip would be done and we could pick up some more supplies in the town, including an ice-cold Coca Cola!

The sinking

Wednesday, 15 June should have been an easy day. The plan was simple: paddle 25km by lunchtime, then rendezvous with the HALO Trust team for a resupply by Kuito Bridge and a well-deserved afternoon off. Gerhard had assigned one of his veterans to look after us: Assistant Provincial Operations Manager Amadeu Bartolomeu Jorge. We were in safe hands. Unfortunately, Angola had other plans for us.

We were also beginning to pass through a section of river that had seen a lot more historic activity than the earlier sections. That morning we passed the point in the river where English explorer Verney Lovett Cameron had crossed in October 1875. He was the first European to cross Equatorial Africa from the Indian Ocean to the Atlantic Ocean. A few years later, in March 1878, the river hosted another explorer, Portuguese administrator Alexandre de Serpa Pinto, as he crossed eastwards from Benguela to Natal. It was amazing for us to think that if things got really desperate, Luanda was only a one-month trek away, as it had been for them.

Around 10km into our journey we heard roaring water. This in itself was not unusual, as we had heard a similar noise back at the first diamond mine we encountered. It just meant fast-flowing water or rapids and that we needed to approach with caution. The obstacle was quite clear: some local fishermen had stretched an A-frame wooden structure out from one side of the river bank to an island in the middle of the river and filled it with fish traps.

The whole thing was 30m wide, with the stretch of river on the other side of the island being only 10m wide, but with a number of rocks. There was a small 1.5m gap in the frame right in the middle where the two sides did not touch. It was an impressive construction, given the fast flow of the water, and they had reinforced it with a number of heavy rocks on top to prevent it washing away. I had no idea how they could have achieved this without a motorised boat.

We paused by the bank and assessed the situation. There were only two options: line ourselves up with the centre of the river to shoot through the gap, or unload the kayak and portage a short distance around it. Going the other way around the island was not feasible, as that looked very shallow and had a number of rocks obstructing the flow which would destroy the Klepper hull. In a move that would have made my kayaking coach Gavin groan, we actually went for a third option: try and paddle from the left bank of the river to the island, parallel to the barrier. We thought we could then assess the obstacle from a closer vantage point, portaging across the island if we needed to.

Hindsight is a wonderful thing. If I had thought back to my training on the fast-flowing River Thames, I would have remembered that crossing from one bank to another pushes you a long way downstream. To avoid this, you traverse the river by pointing your kayak fully upstream and paddling against the current, only slightly steering towards your final destination. If you put the kayak perpendicular to the flow of the water, the water resistance increases exponentially and you just get swept along.

However, I was not thinking about my training. I was thinking about that delicious, ice-cold can of Coke waiting for me only two hours' paddling further downriver from this annoying obstacle. Neither Alfy nor I wanted the hour-plus delay that a portage would create. So we headed for the opposite bank to think of a strategy.

Paddling as hard as we could towards the island, we were dragged sideways straight towards the wooden barrier. We did not even have enough time to turn ourselves to face downstream and try sneaking through the gap before we slammed side-on into the poles. Water immediately began rushing up over the side of the kayak. We were stuck in violent rapids and about to sink.

Both of us jumped out of the kayak onto the barrier, which was luckily so sturdy that it took our weight (with a lot of creaking). Alfy began pulling our rucksacks and other gear off the back of the Klepper and handing them to me, while I ran down the short stretch of barrier and threw them onto the island. As soon as we got out of the kayak, it lost what little remaining stability it had and flipped over, sinking and becoming wedged underwater against the barrier, with the top facing upriver. We watched in horror as the drone, strapped to the front of the Klepper with only an orange survival bag covering it, became fully submerged. Alfy grabbed it and threw it to me. I threw it on the grass of the island and returned for more gear. Our emergency paddle, strapped to the outside of the kayak, floated off down the river. Next went my boots, which had been next to my seat, but not secured to the Klepper. Then one of our water filtration systems was swept away. Next a dry bag. This was rapidly turning into a disaster.

Figure 15 – The Klepper strikes a fishing dam and sinks (15 June 2016)

As we scrambled wildly to salvage what we could from the Klepper, a man in bright-red trousers appeared on a pathway next to the river and ran down, shouting to ask if we needed help. Seeing that we were in trouble, and with no regard for his own safety, he scrambled across the barrier, leaped over the gap and jumped down into the water on the upstream side, trying to help Alfy lift the kayak back out of the water.

The one other detail I remember about the man was that he had a severely withered left arm, with only three fingers. But he was not letting this disability hold him back. Far from it, he recklessly tried to wedge himself between the kayak and the barrier to lift it. We had to force him to move, out of fear that he might slip over, become trapped and drown.

Had this crash occurred in deeper water, the Klepper would no doubt have been lost. But the river was only chest deep in this section, which is probably why the fishermen selected it for their fish traps in the first place. Once we had emptied out the kayak as best we could, Alfy said we had to lift the kayak out of the water and re-float it. This was more easily said than done. Even when empty the Klepper weighed over 40kg, and at the moment it was full of hundreds of kilograms of water, with the full flow of the Kwanza pressing it against the barrier.

The three of us heaved as hard as we could, and with a little fortunate movement of the barrier struts themselves, we got the kayak pointed upstream and re-floated it. Through some miracle, it had not snapped in half and the skin had not been punctured. Serious damage to the skin would have ended our expedition right there, as we did not have a spare one.

The kayak was still half-full of water and very difficult to manoeuvre. Once again, we were faced with two choices. With the current up to our chests and threatening to sweep us away, we quickly discussed a plan. Should we try and haul the kayak over the barrier, then float it down into the calmer waters? Or should we try and keep it parallel to the flow of the water, facing upstream, and slowly walk it horizontally towards the island, which was only about 15m away? We chose the latter option and soon paid for it.

After only a few metres of shimmying, the kayak filled up with water again. Almost in slow motion, she tipped over onto her side and wedged right back up against the barrier, completely underwater. This time the situation was far worse, as the kayak was leaning against only one vertical pole, so the force was not distributed throughout the frame as it had been before. Immediately, the frame buckled. The sound was drowned out by the roar of the rapids, but we all saw there was a lot of snapping going on inside the skin, as the thin wooden skeleton caved under the immense pressure.

Thinking quickly, Alfy moved downstream of the barrier and tried to lift it to relieve some of the pressure on the Klepper. Our Angolan friend stayed at the front with me, trying to pull the nose away from the barrier and face her upstream. The guy was only about five feet five, but he was putting me to shame, hauling at the nose and barking instructions in broken Portuguese at the two of us. I grew increasingly concerned about Alfy being on the downstream side of a sharp and heavy series of wooden stakes and rocks that at any minute could collapse and injure him. I shouted at him to move back onto our side, but my voice was drowned out by the water flow and he was too focused on the heavy lifting to hear. Then he slipped.

Alfy's head briefly vanished underwater. My heart sank in terror. What if he was pinned? My mind flashed back to the horrendous scene in the Liam Neeson thriller *The Grey*, when one of the oil men is trapped under a rock in fast flowing water and drowns right in front of him.

Before I could even jump over the barrier to help, Alfy reappeared, spluttering and in some considerable pain. It looked as though his leg had become trapped underwater. With a grimace and some more lifting, he managed to get free and re-join us on the safer side of the fishing dam.

With the same mixture of brute force and gentle manipulation, the three of us managed to finally re-float the Klepper for a second time. As it came up, I could already see the damage. Some of the central wooden ribs were completely crumpled and the skin was badly misshapen in parts. As far as we could see, there were no punctures. We hauled the kayak up onto the island and took stock of the situation. The scene was one of devastation. Not only was the kayak badly damaged, but all of the gear that we had recovered was waterlogged. Some of the dry bags where we had stored our most delicate electronic equipment were inflated like balloons, water having forced its way inside due to the pressure of the current. As we laid out our clothing to dry, we began checking for missing and destroyed items.

During all this commotion, it was not just the man in the red trousers who had come to our aid. We had not noticed it, but there was a group of three or four boys, spread across both banks, who had been meticulously fishing our possessions out of the water as they were swept away. It brought a smile to our faces at an otherwise difficult time watching this procession of kids march back up the bank carrying our emergency paddle, a couple of dry bags and the water purifier.

With a few hand gestures and some shouting, we established that they could leave the stuff on the far bank and we would collect it later. The man in the red trousers admonished us for damaging his fishing dam, suggested that we pay some money to fix it (which we gladly handed over) and then bid us good luck. As quickly as he had arrived, he skipped back across the river using the fishing dam as a bridge and vanished off into the bush.

Our concern now was getting off this wretched island. The most obvious route was to follow the red-trousered man and carry the gear back across the dam piece by piece, before hiking up the river to find help. My only reservation was that, as the man had pointed out, we had badly damaged the dam in the crash. Pieces of it had already washed away as we were manipulating it to get the Klepper out. While it seemed fine for this small guy, probably about 50kg, to hop over, it might be a different story for us, especially when weighed down with expedition gear. Beyond someone rescuing us in a boat, we did not have much choice, so while Alfy sorted out the kit, dismantled the Klepper and checked what was missing, I strapped on the first rucksack.

The adrenaline was already flowing, so perhaps it did not occur to us what a bad idea this was. As I clambered along the slippery wood on all fours, the fishing dam creaked and sagged under the combined weight of me and an expedition bag. The total weight was over 100kg even before the rucksack was soaked in water. As I reached the gap, I was able to lean across and get a firm handhold before lowering my legs into the fast-flowing channel.

At this point, the added weight was a benefit and my bare feet were firmly planted on the river bed as the current rushed around them. Once on the other side, I rushed across the final 10m wooden section to the safety of the far bank. The relief of having made it was tempered by the fact that Alfy and I would have to repeat this journey four or five more times each to move all of the gear from the island to the mainland. One of the children, who had been sat patiently watching on the bank, offered to head back over with me to fetch the next load. I told him that under no circumstances was he to clamber across that dam.

Regardless of whether or not he could swim, he was so small that the current would surely wash him away if he fell. Instead, he offered to head down the path and fetch us help. As far as I could see, there was nothing but wilderness down the path, but it could not hurt, so I encouraged him along and then headed back over the barrier to talk to Alfy. Despite my reduced weight, the wood creaked even more on the way back. It did not feel stable at all.

'We need to get all this stuff over to that side, then trek to the dam before it gets dark.'

Alfy's matter-of-fact statement was the only call we could make, but I still did not want to hear it.

'I really don't think that barrier is going to stand up to us carrying all the gear across it.'

'We don't have a choice.'

I looked downstream. The water was fast flowing for a while, but emptied out into a deeper, wider section a hundred metres further on. It was not actually a bad spot to clamber out of the water, with shallow banks and overhanging trees that we could grip onto. I remembered reading something about how crocodiles do not like rapids and hoping it was accurate. We began loading up our bags.

Just before we were ready to go, the river made our decision a lot easier. With a snap and an almighty splash, the entire nearside section of the dam collapsed into the river and was swept away at high speed. There were now at least 20m of rapids between us and the surviving section of dam. We had been two minutes away from stepping out onto that doomed structure. Now what?

The answer was that we would need to wade across the other side of the island, through the fast flowing, rocky but ultimately shallower section of river that we had been unable to kayak down. The gear would need to be balanced on our heads. When Alfy first suggested this, I thought he was mad, but again, we had no choice. Only a boat with an engine could access us on the island, and I had not seen one of those for our entire journey. I suggested trying to throw some of our lighter gear over to the other side, to reduce the total number of trips. Although the bank was steeper, it was only about 10m away. Alfy grabbed the spare tyre from the buggy and launched it into the air. It landed just short and floated off down the river. So much for that idea.

With our precious gear on our heads, we set out across the river. The river bed was uneven and rocky and the depth highly variable. Alfy, being three inches taller and a lot more athletic, had a much better time of the crossing than me. On a couple of occasions, I was faced with the unenviable choice of letting go of the gear or ending up with my head underwater. In the end, we came up with a relay system, using the rock outcrops as waypoints, to help us get everything safely to the other side. We then walked all the gear down a well-trodden path, to see what we would find at the next bend of the river. This is where we met Isaías.

Isaías was an older gentleman, probably in his late fifties. He wore a battered khaki sun hat with a frayed rim, the type you see hunters wearing in South Africa. His t-shirt was brown and faded, with the words 'VS-Basic' emblazoned on the front in dirty white lettering. Alfy and I both commented on his fine pair of grey suit trousers, which seemed a little out of place given his profession. After greeting us warmly, Isaías expressed his condolences for our misfortune. He had seen what had happened to us, but had been powerless to help.

'*Muita confusão!*' He shook his head solemnly.

Isaías was the local ferry master. He stood at the helm of a battered dual-hulled dugout canoe, complete with a rusty shovel for a paddle. The shovel had a hole in the middle of the metal face. I have no idea how he had done it, but somehow, he had fused together two dugouts into a wider, catamaran-type configuration. Both the front and back were full of holes, some of which he had repaired with mud. There were a few pieces of scrap metal holding the back section together. Isaías told us that twice a day it was his job to move people from one side of the river to the other.

'Who comes down here and uses your services?' We were both puzzled.

'The miners. They work a few kilometres further down, but they all live over in that village.' He pointed off down one of the pathways.

We were still struggling to understand the economics of his business. 'How much do people pay you to cross?'

THE SINKING

Figure 16 – Isaías the ferry master

'They pay nothing. The diamond mine pays me to be here. I receive two thousand kwanzas per month.'

Even using the official exchange rate, this was a derisory amount (about twelve dollars per month). Given the decline in the oil price and the recent inflation, in real terms, this amounted to less than four dollars per month. All for a job that required him to be on duty for a good few hours every morning and evening. Isaías kindly offered to ferry our bags over the river, as the side we had crossed to was not the side of the diamond mine, where he suggested we would most likely find help.

'How much weight can she take?' I nodded towards the ancient canoe.

'Oh, don't worry. Very strong! You can both get in! And your gear!'

Alfy and I were sceptical. It would be an ironic twist to save all of our gear from treacherous rapids only to lose it 100m further down the river in a perfectly still stretch of water. In the end, we stuck both of our rucksacks into the front and I clambered on top. Alfy decided to stay on the bank to prepare the next load. We lent Isaías a proper paddle to speed up the process. He was amazed by the lightweight Werner paddle. It was a shame we did not have a second spare or we could have left it for him. It was definitely better than a shovel with a hole in it.

We set off across the river and immediately got into trouble. Either the canoe was overloaded or we had not distributed the weight correctly. Either way, I soon found myself bailing frantically, while Isaías tried to turn us around and get back to the bank as quickly as possible. At one stage he even chucked me a wet rag to fix one of the new holes that had just sprung up in the side of his vessel. The whole thing would have been comical, but sinking the source of a man's livelihood when he was doing us a favour would have been a terrible end to the day. Once we were close enough to the bank, I threw Alfy my rucksack, which alleviated some of the pressure on the hull and we managed to get back safely.

Over the next hour we watched Isaías patiently shuttle one item at a time over the river, leaving it in a neat pile on the opposite bank. Once Alfy and I had been safely deposited on the side of the diamond mine, he bid us farewell, without any suggestion of payment. We offered him two thousand kwanzas (around four dollars) as it was the smallest note we were carrying on the expedition (for emergencies only). He eventually accepted, before paddling off back down the river, looking for his regular fares. It was 5pm already. We had under two hours to come up with a plan before darkness fell.

By now, word of our sinking had spread far and wide. Afrikaners talk about this system of word of mouth news as the 'bush radio'. One of the children who retrieved our gear must have run down to the diamond mine and informed the workers there. Before we knew it, a short man named Alexandre was on the scene. He was about our age, with a finely trimmed moustache, grey Samford basketball t-shirt and a white cap. His well-ironed jeans and polished jet-black shoes hinted at his status. These were not shoes that one waded in the mud with. Alexandre was obviously not your regular *garimpeiro*.

'My friends, are you OK? I came as soon as I heard. What a terrible disaster.'

We reassured him that beyond a few bumps and scratches, we were both fine.

'You must come with me to Camacupa tonight, this is where we are based. We can make a plan to get you help tomorrow morning.'

With a quick whistle, we were suddenly surrounded by more children, who came sprinting out of the bushes and grabbed our piles of gear. Picking up the heavy kayak bags ourselves, we put our faith in Alexandre and followed him in a Pied Piper-like procession along the side of the river. Three kilometres later, we reached the mine that everyone had been talking about. Here, a set of heavy earth-moving machinery had been used to dam off a meander in the river and then all the water had been pumped out. Legions of muddy workers had just finished their shift down on the river bed, digging out the sediment and hauling it back up the banks in large sacks, to be filtered by hand nearby using sieves. The smell of diesel and the bulldozed expanse of wilderness was a jarring contrast to our earlier isolation.

Alexandre had all of our gear thrown in the back of a Toyota Hilux, and we clambered on board. It was a 60km drive to the town of Camacupa, much of it on dirt roads (a minimum of two days of trekking if we had not been rescued). His driver, a heavy-set man with a booming laugh, found the whole situation surreal. He kept asking about the Klepper: where was it? Did it have an engine? Were we not worried about all the wildlife on the river? He could not get past our lack of an engine.

'Why don't you buy an outboard motor in Camacupa? Your journey will be much quicker!'

He was not joking. Like many of the Angolans we met, the idea of undertaking such a journey for no commercial gain, in a slow and inefficient means of transportation, was baffling. We explained that we were doing the journey to help the HALO Trust with their mine clearance work in Angola. While there was immediate recognition of the charity down in this part of Angola, our motives were still a little unclear to most.

After an hour of driving we arrived in Camacupa. The town is just to the south of the Luando Nature Reserve, which straddles the border between Bié and Malanje Provinces. Camacupa is on Angola's former Benguela Railway, which connected the ports of Benguela and Lobito to the vast mineral wealth of the Congo's Katanga Province. It was founded in 1921 and was known as Vila General Machado under Portuguese rule.

During the civil war, the infrastructure in this part of the country was badly damaged, beginning with the railway line. In recent years the Angolan government has made efforts to rehabilitate the line, and in January 2012 a newly minted Chinese train made the journey from Huambo to Camacupa. If things got really bad, we could always take the train back to Luanda from here.

Despite its new rail connection, the place still feels like a frontier town. The main avenue is a wide, dusty mud road. On both sides the pavements are adorned with neatly clipped trees and succulents. MPLA bunting flaps in the wind between street lighting. A few buildings, such as the bright-pink cultural centre, look new, with corrugated iron roofs and freshly painted signage. Many of the street-front houses look as though they have not been maintained since the 1960s. An old eight-tower silo dominates the skyline in the centre of town, sitting abandoned by the side of the railway line that cuts through town.

The street where Alexandre took us had thin strips of tarmac left on the road, hints that it was once paved. Most of the houses were single storey, with neatly painted white and green facades. The roofs sported traditional Portuguese terracotta tiling. All the signs indicated that this was once a prosperous mining and trading town, but those days had long passed. With the connection to Katanga severed, there was little reason for anyone to come this far east from the coast now, unless they were hunting for diamonds.

We settled into a local bar. The TV was blasting some sort of Angolan talent show, but the beers were cold. Just next door, Alexandre maintained a basic apartment where his mining managers and engineers could stay when rotating into and out of the bush camps. There was no question of us finding a hotel. He insisted that we crash with them that night.

Alexandre showed a lot more interest in the logistics of our journey than anyone else we had met. While we sat together in the bar, Alfy explained how we had arrived at Camacupa and how we intended to continue our journey. Alexandre, who had travelled for tens of kilometres downriver on the hunt for new diamond concessions, patiently mapped out the obstacles that we would face and which side of the river we should get out to portage around them.

'You must beware of *sete ilhas* (seven islands). This is a serious obstacle, with many waterfalls, up ahead. Miners I know have lost motorboats there.'

Alexandre could not show us exactly where *sete ilhas* was, but we noted down his warning nonetheless.

Figure 17 – Route planning with Alexandre (15 June 2016)

That evening I got on the satellite phone to Gerhard at the HALO Trust and explained the situation. He was incredibly supportive.

'Listen, guys, whatever we need to do to help you finish, I will make it happen. Amadeu is there to help. You just say the word.'

He told us that Amadeu and his driver Firmino would meet us in the town the following morning, complete with a food resupply that Gerhard himself had picked up from a supermarket in Huambo. We could make a plan directly with them. This was great news.

From back in London it must have seemed as though our trip was grinding to a halt. Our website location had not been updated and even our ever-supportive girlfriends had started to doubt we would be coming home with the trip complete.

After a brief chat with all the other engineers staying in our flat, Alfy and I passed out in our room, exhausted, frustrated but ultimately relieved at the way the day had ended.

On the morning of Thursday, 16 June we had a lot of work to do if we were to have any hope of finishing by the Monday, 11 July deadline. Amadeu and Firmino arrived early, having driven 250km over rough roads to reach us from their base in Huambo. We had already met Amadeu briefly at the HALO base in Huambo. He struck me as cool, calm and collected. The more we got to know each other, the more he reinforced this view. As an older Angolan, he had lived through the war in the central highlands, one of the most badly affected parts of the country. He was a deeply religious man, keen to work hard to improve the lives of his countrymen. Always friendly, it was great to have him by our side as we negotiated the difficulties ahead.

As we met Amadeu that morning, he was in high spirits as always, thanking God that we had been delivered safely from the sinking. Although none of our new mining friends knew him, they had heard of the HALO Trust, and Amadeu's calm but serious manner elicited a natural respect from everyone he introduced himself to. Poor Firmino was very ill, lying in the passenger seat of the HALO Land Rover, trying to keep as still as possible. Firmino was pretty dour at the best of times, so his current condition was not helping his mood. I poked my head into the Land Rover window, and with some effort he turned his head to look at me. His bloodshot eyes blinked slowly.

'Are you OK, Firmino? You look terrible!'

He did not respond.

'We think it is *paladismo*,' Amadeu said in a concerned tone.

The sinking

Although the technical Portuguese translation of *paladismo* is malaria, in central Angola this term seems to be used more broadly for many types of ailments that show similar symptoms to malaria (such as fever and a headache). Back in Luanda, most expatriate employers would have treated this as a medical emergency. According to the World Health Organization, over 2.7 million Angolans were infected with malaria in 2015, with an estimated 14,000 deaths. In this part of the country, *paladismo* was just a fact of daily life, something to be put up with, unless things got really bad.

Alfy laid out the Klepper on the pavement outside our flat. The few passing pedestrians were curious as to what these two foreigners were doing with an assortment of snapped wooden parts and what looked like a deflated boat. Our initial damage assessment was bad: a third of the wooden parts that constituted the frame of the Klepper were snapped or otherwise damaged. This included one of the two key metal-hinged struts that ran the length of the Klepper and gave it rigidity in rough water. Thankfully, even on closer inspection there was no major damage to the canvas skin. Alfy and Amadeu headed off to find a carpenter capable of fixing the Klepper while I drove off with Firmino in the HALO Trust Land Rover on a shopping trip around Camacupa, looking to replace some of our gear that had sunk to the bottom of the Kwanza.

It was a surreal experience shoe shopping in central Angola. I do not enjoy shopping at the best of times, but this was important. My hiking boots had been one of the first casualties in the sinking, and without replacements the upcoming portage sections were going to be impossible. I tried two building supply stores, both run by Lebanese merchants, but one was out of stock and the other only had work boots going up to UK size 10 (European 44.5). My feet are UK size 11 (European 46) and could hardly fit into these boots, let alone hike long distances carrying weight. In the end, we stumbled across a small concrete store selling clothes, that also had a few pairs of shoes. Five minutes later, I was the proud owner of a pair of Nike Air Jordans of dubious origin. They were size 10.5, which was as good as I was going to get. For some reason, everyone in this part of the world had smaller feet.

A quick trip to the central market to fetch Alfy a new fleece and pair of khaki trousers and we were in business. Most of the stall holders only had military print clothing, which would not have helped us in our interaction with the Angolan authorities, but eventually I found Alfy a dashing orange fleece and trousers. We were going to be the most stylish people on the river.

I returned to our temporary accommodation to find Alfy surrounded by a crowd of people on the pavement, all deep in discussion. Crouched by the shattered Klepper parts was our saviour: Zé. He had some experience with woodwork from making coffins and had also done a bit of welding and riveting in his friend's car garage. He sounded perfect for the job.

'How much will it cost to fix all the parts?'

'Six thousand kwanzas?' He was almost sheepish with his response.

This was less than forty dollars using the official exchange rate. Although this was a very unusual job, by the sound of his voice he felt like he was overcharging, but Alfy and I would have paid ten times that just to get back out on the river quickly.

'OK, and we'll double it if you can get it done by this evening and do a good job!' Alfy said.

Zé was delighted, but not confident he could complete the work by that evening.

Figure 18 – Alfy and Zé fixing the Klepper in Camacupa

We left him to it, gathered up our gear and headed back to the point where we had sunk the kayak. Alfy and I wanted to hike the 16km stretch of river from the point where we sank to the point at the Kuito Bridge where we had originally planned to meet the HALO Trust vehicle for a resupply. That way, there would be no gaps in our source to sea journey.

It was a pleasant enough walk that afternoon, although we made two mistakes. Firstly, we set out too late, mainly due to all the messing around in Camacupa that morning, trying to find Zé. The sun set about 10km into our walk, but thankfully a lot of it was on marked tracks and there were a fair amount of people around due to our proximity to Camacupa. The second mistake was my decision to walk in the fake Nike Air Jordans I had bought earlier on that day.

There had really been no alternative, but hiking in shoes that are too small for you is bound to lead to problems. Sure enough, about 5km in I began to feel rubbing on the pads of both feet. Over the next 6km this minor inconvenience grew into something quite noticeable, and by the time we arrived at our destination and I took the trainers off, both feet were badly blistered. I thought nothing of it at the time, but this initially small injury was to cause me major problems later on in the expedition.

At 6.30pm our dirt track hit a main road. Up ahead we could hear the river and see the dark shadow that was the Kuito Bridge; our original target for the previous day. Amadeu had told us to look out for an army base, where he had organised with the commander for us to stay the night. In the morning, he would bring the newly repaired Klepper over to our location, and we would carry it down to the river and continue our journey. At least, this was the plan.

Kuito Bridge was a bit of a misnomer, as Kuito city was actually 90km to the south-west, but this was the nearest major settlement on most maps and it was the administrative capital of the province we were in (Bié Province). On 6 January 1993, following the breakdown of the Bicesse Accords, UNITA began a nine-month siege of Kuito. The town was completely cut off from the rest of Angola and the citizens starved. Over 30,000 people died, many of whom are buried in a large cemetery on the outskirts of the city.

Kuito hit the international headlines in 1995 thanks to an image taken by Mines Advisory Group photographer Sean Sutton, called 'A Long Walk Home'. It shows two Angolan men, both on crutches having lost a leg to landmines, walking up a long hill in the central Angolan city. Landmine clean-up efforts continue around the city to this day.

Figure 19 – Graves in Kuito (March 2012)

My first question was how on earth Amadeu had managed to persuade the Angolan Armed Forces (*Forças Armadas Angolanas*: FAA) to sign off on us camping on their base. The answer was simple: this was no ordinary military base, but a forward operating base for the Angolan military's own demining wing, the *Instituto Nacional de Desminagem* (INAD). They had an excellent working relationship with the HALO Trust and were all too happy to help in our efforts to publicise their cause.

The base was to the side of the unlit main strip that headed into the nearby settlement by Chinquala, confusingly called Cuanza village. We could see a group of soldiers sat around a camp fire in the parade ground, surrounded by a variety of tents, mud-brick structures and two semi-rigid hangars. We wandered in, careful to make as much noise as possible so as not to sneak up on the men with rifles.

After five years of living in Angola, my experience of interacting with the FAA was still very limited. Beyond being cut up by their trucks in the snarling Luanda traffic, we had not had much to do with each other. My general impressions from travelling around Africa were that it would be wise to keep it this way, but in this instance, I was very wrong.

The commander could not have been friendlier, telling us to throw our bags in the hangar and make ourselves at home. There were only seven or eight men on the base that night, as the rest were forward deployed clearing nearby minefields. We therefore had our pick of the tents. After a brief round of introductions around the fire, I got straight down to business:

'Does anyone here have some large boots they would like to sell me?'

There was some hushed discussion amongst the troops, then they shouted for one of their comrades to come over. Out of the shadows appeared a giant of a man, in full military uniform. He strode over and shook my hand.

'I need shoes to protect my feet while hiking. These ones are no good. You have large feet; can you sell me some boots?'

His eyes lit up as I explained my dilemma.

'Give me one minute!'

He vanished back to his tent, then reappeared with a very sad-looking pair of black boots. This was promising. They looked big enough.

'These will fit you. Try them, try them!'

I promptly ruined my negotiating position by trying them on and then shouting for joy that they were the right fit.

'How much do you want for them?' I tried to sound disinterested.

The man looked at the other troops and grinned. He crossed his arms then turned to me.

'Give me twenty thousand kwanzas. Then they are yours.'

At the official exchange rate, this was over $120, an outrageous amount. Even at the black-market rate, it was too much for a worn old pair of boots.

'I'll give you three thousand kwanzas. These are not new boots after all!'

A wave of laughter spread throughout the group of soldiers. 'This one likes to bargain!' one of them shouted, slapping his friend on the back. A brief round of haggling later, and the boots were mine, for the bargain price of four thousand five hundred kwanzas.

We all sat round the fire together that evening. The soldiers were eating their traditional *funge*, a plain carbohydrate made from cassava flour (*fufu*), with the same consistency as mashed potato. I was never a big fan of the flavour, but *funge* is incredibly popular nationwide. At our staff Christmas dinner at Luanda International School, I used to watch some Angolan members of staff load up their plates with the stuff, to the exclusion of all the other food on offer. On this occasion, there was not enough *funge* to go around anyway, so Alfy and I cooked up a chorizo sausage in silver foil with rice.

Our Trangia (a Swedish portable stove) was a hit with the soldiers, who wished they had something like that for making coffee in the morning. After dinner, all the soldiers wandered off into town, leaving us as the only people on the base. We thought this was an odd move considering that we were foreign, but were glad for the vote of confidence. There was no word from the carpenter all evening. That night, we slept in one of the hangars, a space that could normally fit 20 troops. A surreal end to another surreal day.

On Friday, 17 June we were awoken by a cockerel that had wandered onto the parade ground. The phone rang as we were having breakfast. It was Amadeu, and he had bad news:

'The carpenter is not sure he can finish the work today. You will have to wait there.'

This was not what we wanted to hear after two days of delays. We were 50 or 60km behind schedule, and if we sat in the base another night, that deficit would grow to over 100km. Amadeu promised us an update by 10am. So in the ensuing two hours, we decided to use our time productively by reducing the weight we were carrying. The hike from the sinking site had shown us that we had far too much gear for long sections of portage, especially if the pathway was too narrow to construct the buggy. We needed to be ruthless with our weight allowances. At the start of the trip, each of our bags was at about 25kg, plus another 1 or 2kg of water on top. We then had all of the Klepper, the buggy and a load of electronics for filming the journey. It was too much bulk.

The first casualty of the gear cull was the drone. While the footage it had taken thus far had been beautiful, it was too bulky and would be lucky to survive a second dunking in the Kwanza. We threw it in the discard pile, to be handed over to the HALO Trust for safe-keeping. Joining it were several other smaller electronic items, my bulky Canon EOS 450d DSLR camera, adapters, notebooks, maps, parts of the medical kit, a significant proportion of our clothing and some of our rations. We managed to dump a good 6kg of gear without losing anything mission-critical.

Gerhard had very kindly agreed to organise one more resupply meeting with the Land Rover between this section and the next large waypoint, which was Malanje Bridge by Cangandala. We arranged to meet near Lúbia, halfway through our kayak along the Luando Nature Reserve. This meant that we only needed to carry five days' worth of rations, which reduced our total weight further.

Gerhard had picked us up a veritable bounty of supplies from the Shoprite in Huambo, a South African supermarket near the HALO Trust HQ. Chorizo, peanuts, Jelly Tots, jelly beans, dried fruits, spam, noodles, rice, spicy spaghetti and canned tuna. Added to the dehydrated rations we already had, it looked as though we were going to eat well for the rest of the trip.

This delay also meant Alfy and I could finally communicate our revised schedule to the outside world. Thus far our only contact had been a nightly text message containing our GPS coordinates, sent to an automated system that then updated our marker position on our website. We also had to text Harriet back in Huambo to ensure she knew where to send the rescue party, in the event of the emergency plan being activated.

That morning I had a difficult conversation with my girlfriend Steph, who was having a tough time back in London without me. The combination of my prolonged absence and lack of contact, along with the sinking, was stressing out many of our loved ones back home. A couple of times Alfy and I had discussed the pressures of being the ones left behind. We had agreed to avoid alarmist messages home about the crash so as not to worry people too much, especially Alfy's father, who he said was very concerned about the whole enterprise.

I finished my phone conversation with Steph and asked Alfy how his girlfriend had reacted to news of the trip.

'What did Marie-Louise think about this whole trip? Was she enthusiastic about you vanishing off for such a long period of time?'

'It must be a little different for Steph and Marie-Louise. I mean, Marie-Louise is only a day or so away in a 4×4 if she really wants to come and see us later in the expedition. Steph is thousands of kilometres away. But yes, it was still a tough sell.'

'So, what persuaded her in the end then?'

'Well, I'm not sure there was much persuasion. But she knew that I really wanted to do this and I would not be happy if I did not achieve it. She could tell that I was going to do this trip whether she was on board or not. So I guess she didn't want to stand in the way of that.'

I admired Alfy's single-mindedness, but felt bad about what everyone back home might be going through.

As promised, at 10am Amadeu did call, but he had no firm news. Perhaps he would know more that afternoon. Or perhaps we would have to spend the night. We did not want to wait and find out, so we packed up our gear (including the undamaged sections of the Klepper) and hiked out of the camp to find a new entry point to the river. This was a good opportunity to test out our new lighter-weight set-up and also see the kind of water obstacles the fixed Klepper would be facing.

We had a few issues navigating, due to an inaccurate scale on one of the maps we were using (at least, this is what we told ourselves later). What we thought would be a relaxed 10km jaunt through the agricultural hinterland of Chinquala's periphery turned into a 20km slog in brutal midday heat. We occasionally found respite in the shade of a patch of forest, but generally we were walking along exposed paths. Once again, we had issues with interpreting local people's advice on where we were going and how far we had left to trek.

'Which way is the Kwanza River?'
'It is over that way.'
'How far is it?'
'Not far. Less than a day.'

In one village, we appeared to stumble right into the middle of a domestic legal dispute. The *soba* (village elder), identifiable by his trilby hat and smart jacket, was sat on a chair in what we assume was the courtyard of his house. To one side, he had a lady, shouting and gesticulating wildly. On the other, was a man, sat on the floor, shaking his head in displeasure at whatever she was saying. We traipsed past, waving politely to the *soba*. He smiled back then returned his attention to the dispute in front of him. The woman was so busy denouncing the man she did not even notice us.

After three hours of hiking, we came out into a larger clearing with a very neatly laid-out village. The paths had been swept of all debris and the bases of the trees were all painted white, a sub-Saharan African tradition of disputed origin. We spotted a makeshift bench behind one of the mud brick buildings and grabbed a seat in the shade. Quickly, an audience appeared.

First a few children wandered over, staring intently as we drank from our increasingly clogged water filtration bottles. Then the adults began streaming back into the settlement for lunch. As we sat there asking for directions, it felt like we were holding court. A few of the teenagers offered to carry our bags for us. Our refusal to accept help confused a lot of people, but they mainly thought we were strange rather than rude.

It took a while for us to admit it, but we were totally lost. From what we could make out, we were in a meander on the Kwanza, with the river on three sides. But it was impossible to work out which section we should head to in order to avoid a waterfall that everyone told us was present on this stretch. Luckily, after another hour of guessing our way forwards, we picked up some phone signal and Amadeu got in touch with us.

'The repairs are complete! Where are you? We will bring the Klepper to you.'

It was difficult, especially over a crackly line, but eventually Alfy had zeroed in on our location. Just before nightfall, the HALO Trust Land Rover appeared down one of the paths, with Firmino looking just as unwell as he had the day before. It did not help that he had just been bounced around doing some serious off-road driving to get to our position.

Amadeu was immediately on top of the situation, addressing the adults around us in the local language of Umbundu. From a few brief sections of Portuguese, I could hear them discussing the work HALO had done in the area and how it was important that the local community kept an eye on us that evening. It turned out that we only needed to trek down a nearby hill and we would hit a beach on the river that put us clear of the waterfall. Oddly, we noticed that there was another passenger in the Land Rover: it was Zé!

He had delayed a journey to Luanda that day in order to complete the repairs and wanted to talk us through them personally before taking his pay. Alfy inspected each piece by torchlight and gave it the all clear. It was a miracle what Zé had achieved in such a short space of time with only some extra bits of wood, cut metal and a few rivets. While the inspection was being carried out, Amadeu asked one of the children, called Isaac, to guide me down to the river and show us a safe entry point. As we walked down the hill, Isaac was joined by an extremely drunk relative with a fancy hat.

'Do you like sugar cane?' he asked insistently, slurring his words.

I nodded, trying hard not to engage. His eyes were glazed over and he was practically drooling. Whatever he had been drinking, it was strong, and the smell of it wafted on his breath as he leaned in close to me.

'Do yooooooou like sugar cane?'

The next thing I knew, he had stumbled off into the bushes and returned with a long stem that he snapped over his knee.

'Here you go. It's... It's great.'

I accepted the gift, unsure whose sugar cane this was and whether the man was supposed to be trampling through their field. Soon we heard the familiar roar of water and the path opened out onto a pristine white-sand beach, at a point on the river known locally as *Ilha* (island). The drunk man yelled some instructions at Isaac, then stumbled back off up the path to tell Alfy where we were. The child raced around the beach and within five minutes had ignited a large fire, all seemingly without the use of a cigarette lighter or matches. His bush craft skills put us to shame. Then just like that Isaac had also vanished.

Alfy soon appeared down the path and told me that Amadeu, Firmino and Zé had jumped back in the Land Rover and headed off. They had a long drive ahead of them to get back to Huambo and needed to check the roads to see if it was even possible to meet us at Lúbia in a few days. We set up camp on the sand, sweeping the beach for firewood and doing a quick check for crocodile or hippo tracks. It was a noisy place to camp, as the waterfall was just upstream, but we did not care. We were back on the water and ready to start the second section of our expedition: the long journey to Malanje Bridge, near Cangandala.

Rapids and hippos

On Saturday, 18 June we started as early as possible. There was a lot of ground to make up. In our original planning, we had divided the journey up into three stages: from the source to Kuito Bridge, then from Kuito Bridge to Malanje Bridge, and finally from Malanje Bridge to the Atlantic Ocean. This second section we were embarking on now featured some highly isolated stretches and at least 17 sets of rapids. If we got into trouble here, there would be little chance of the HALO Trust Land Rover getting to us. We would need to radio Luanda for a bush pilot and hope he could land somewhere nearby. To further complicate matters, private planes could not get clearance to fly at night, so we could only hope for help during daylight hours. Over the next few days our aim was to get to the mining town of Dando (not to be confused with Dondo), right on the border between Bié and Malanje Provinces.

The low mist hanging over the water at sunrise was quite spectacular, slowly snaking downstream with the water flow. We were back to it being very, very cold. Here the river really widened out, up to 100m. The landscape was also a little more varied, with a selection of trees growing right up to the river banks. Trees meant firewood and easier tent pitching, which was great. Sadly, there were also wide patches of reeds, which meant more hippos. We saw two or three small pods over the course of the day's paddling, but managed to avoid them all successfully. That afternoon we could see two towering plumes of smoke in the distance: further evidence of bush fires.

One favourite topic of conversation on this stretch was explorers, specifically Victorian explorers. Alfy is an avid reader and it was a rich vein for discussion and debate: was Henry Morton Stanley a racist? Would we have liked to be managed by Robert Falcon Scott on an Antarctic expedition? Should David Livingstone have accepted help from the very slave traders he was trying to put out of business? What was Richard Francis Burton thinking when he snuck into Mecca? Had John Hanning Speke committed suicide?

A key point for discussion was whether there was a common

personality trait or background or mental imbalance that united all these explorers. What made them want to do the things that they did?

'I think exploration and expedition travel is an inherently selfish act. I mean, you do ask a lot of other people in order to be successful at something like this,' said Alfy.

I nodded in agreement. 'Yes, and it's odd how it only seems to attract a certain type of personality. I mean, pretty unstable personalities.'

'I can see why the Angolans don't really get this trip. I mean, it doesn't sound like much fun, does it? Didn't one of Scott's men write that this kind of thing is the most isolated way of having a bad time which has been devised?'

'Ha, I'm not sure that I agree but that's a great quotation!'

We established no firm conclusions, beyond agreeing that exploration often seemed to be selfish, satisfying some internal need rather than a wider societal one. Both of us wondered how much of this expedition had been about helping the HALO Trust and how much had been about us simply wanting to get out here.

In total we managed 50km of travel that day, including two small portages around rapids. That evening we found an excellent landing spot on an open, grass-free section of bank, that allowed us to drag the Klepper out of the water to check for leaks. As we were setting up camp, it soon became apparent that we were not alone as a small crowd began to wander over from a diamond camp in a nearby copse.

Everyone was very friendly, and soon a group of ten of us were sat on a nearby log, chatting about what had brought us to this isolated spot. All the men were Angolan and came from every corner of the country. One older man, Nelson, was the self-designated spokesman of the group. Nelson was small, likely stunted by malnutrition during childhood. His face was old beyond his years, with deep furrows in his cheeks and brow from working out in the Angolan sun every day. He told us about the hardships they were facing out in the bush:

'We have been here for three months and still no money. We have found nothing in this area, so the boss, he doesn't pay us. But we have invested so much to come here, leaving our families, paying for transport, for diesel, for food. We must find something.'

Nelson outlined their typical work day – they would get up with the dawn, scrape together some *funge* for breakfast, then get out on the water as early as possible. They had a rudimentary pontoon which was attached to a wire cable, slung across the river. The pontoon had a diesel pump on board and a length of hosing, which a diver would use to suck up sediment from the river bed. When he said diver, he did not mean a man with SCUBA gear, but simply an unfortunate worker who had to brave the icy water with little more than a length of garden hose attached to a compressor to breathe through, or even just a snorkel. Once they had enough sediment, they would take it back to the bank in big sandbags, to be filtered by hand through a set of sieves.

It was dirty, dangerous work, alternating between freezing in the mornings and sweltering in the midday heat. Their living quarters looked like a makeshift refugee camp. The lucky ones had tents. Others were left to fashion rain protection from whatever they could find: felled branches, tarpaulin, even canvas from the sediment sacks themselves.

'This is not good work. If we do not find diamonds in the next three weeks, we must move down the river. But perhaps you can help us.'

With that, Nelson shuffled off the bench and reappeared five minutes later with something in his hand. It was a long, hexagonal piece of rock, perfectly smooth on every side. It was dark by this stage, but by the firelight the rock looked pitch black, like a piece of black quartz.

'We keep finding these things in the river. Do you know what they are? Are they valuable?'

Neither Alfy nor I had any idea. Apparently, there are indicator minerals that you find in diamond-rich earth, but whether or not this mysterious black rock was one of them was anyone's guess. Nelson shrugged and put the object back in his pocket.

I moved the discussion on to one of my favourite topics. 'Does anyone have a pair of large shoes they want to sell me? European size 46?' My army boots were already letting me down, causing large blisters.

This led to a 10-minute debate among the miners as to why I had such big feet and what was wrong with my very old army boots. Eventually one of them said he 'knew a guy'. Off he ran back to their camp and then, sure enough, a man appeared holding a pair of fake Italian leather loafers. Hardly ideal hiking shoes, but they fit perfectly. I snapped them up. With a roaring fire, fine company and even finer Italian footwear, morale was back at an all-time high that night. We even noticed that we had camped with a bees' nest in the tree above us, but the smoke from our fire seemed to keep them calm. We went to sleep to the sound of their gentle buzzing.

Sunday, 19 June was a big day. We knew that there would be two long sections of portage before we arrived in Dando, hopefully on Monday evening. The satellite photography was not clear on exactly how much of the river was navigable, but we knew we would face a few sections of hiking, up to 15km at a time. We set off in good time and managed 35km of uninterrupted paddling before we were due to hit our first obstacle: a violent series of rapids.

We never actually saw them, but thanks to Alfy's careful route planning, knew exactly where they were and where to get out to avoid them. Just to double-check, we asked another local ferry captain. He had chosen a calm section of the river to ply his trade on, about 50m wide, with gentle sloping banks on either side. No issues with mooring at either end and definitely nowhere for hippos to sneak up on him. He had a long, thin dugout canoe that he pushed along using a wooden pole, half punting, half paddling. We coasted up next to him, on the side of the river we thought we needed to get out on to begin the hike.

'Good morning, sirs,' he said, in his best Portuguese. 'Where have you come from?'

As we explained our situation, he became more and more animated, expressing his surprise with increasingly loud shouts of 'eh!' as we spoke. While all this was going on, a group of men carrying machetes and women with various items balanced on their heads arrived at the far bank.

'Get over here!' yelled one of the waiting men impatiently. 'We need a lift across!'

Annoyed by the interruption, the ferry captain did not even turn to face them.

'Shut your mouths!'

He was clearly busy talking to us. Fearing causing a village revolt, we bid him farewell and hauled the Klepper up onto the bank. He drifted off towards the passengers.

'I'm coming, I'm coming! Shut up!'

Our landing site seemed to be a clothes-washing spot, and there were still suds floating in the water next to the worn-down log that was used for scrubbing the clothes. A path led off up the hill to the village. As we were unloading the kayak and began stripping off the skin from the hull, a couple of women arrived. Then a few more. Then some children. Before we knew it, we had an audience of 40 or 50 people as we packed up the gear ready for the hike.

People were wearing an interesting mixture of African fabrics and Western clothing. One little five-year-old stared at us suspiciously, wearing an Italian national football team away kit from the mid '90s. The men were all dressed in long trousers, mainly jeans, despite the heat. Alfy did his best magician routine, pulling apart the Klepper with a flourish to 'oohs' and 'aahs' from the crowd.

Soon, we were all packed down and ready to march into the bush. But first, we needed water. My instinct was to fill up where we were standing. If our water filters could clear out cholera, presumably they could also remove soap suds. But everyone around us shook their heads. There was better water up in the village. We had to follow them up the hill to grab some. We trudged up the path, with the Klepper split between us in our hiking bags, through a series of cultivated fields. I could see bananas, what looked like cassava and even a few chilli plants.

Soon, the path opened out into the village, which was neatly laid out on a north–south axis around a large cleared central area, dominated by a *jango*. The houses were single-entrance mud brick with thatch roofs. We were led to one of the larger houses, which was used to store water in big clay urns (along with a few plastic bins). The children were not allowed in this room, but the adults showed us it was clean by gulping down mouthfuls from a jug. The water was cool and looked delicious. Alfy and I would have killed to copy the men and guzzle a refreshing pint, but we could not risk getting ill. We filled up our water bladders and the filtration bottles and resigned ourselves to slowly sucking the water through a very thin straw. The Water-to-Go bottles look just like your regular 750ml sports bottles, but there is a complicated filter attached to the head, which you must pull the water through using suction. The dirtier the water, the slower the flow rate. Sometimes it would take a good 20 seconds of suction to get half a mouthful of water. It was so frustrating.

The men of the village were sat around the *jango*, doing nothing in particular. A couple of mangy-looking dogs sat around, flicking their ears to keep the flies away. It would have been great to camp here for the night, but we had a hike to get on with. Alfy took his GPS out and started asking questions about a route to a re-entry point past the rapids. Many of the men grunted in disinterest, laid prone by a day of heavy drinking.

I took this opportunity to tape up my feet as best I could. The army boots I had bought had been very uncomfortable and probably caused more problems than they had solved. The blisters on both feet had expanded across both pads. I was going to attempt the hike today in a combination of thick socks, gauze dressing held on by micropore tape and my Italian leather loafers. As far as I could tell it would be a flat walk along single-track paths in the forest. Not too taxing on the footwear, but also not enough space to construct the buggy, so we would have to carry all of the Klepper's weight.

Thanks to the requirements of Guinness World Records, we were unable to follow in the footsteps of Henry Morton Stanley and offload all of our gear on a vast baggage train of local porters. Alfy had also neglected to bring his litter, so we could not be carried along in luxury for this segment (a mode of transport perhaps more befitting his allegedly royal appearance). However, without space for the buggy we simply could not carry all of the gear. We therefore made the decision to carry the Klepper and associated parts ourselves and ask some of the local lads to help by carrying other items (such as supplies and clothing).

This suggestion did not go down too well with the lads sat in the *jango*, who seemed to be gearing up for an afternoon of drinking more Best Whisky and socialising. Best Whisky, despite its name, is actually a filthy brew whose flavour has less in common with whisky than it does with paint stripper. While you can buy it in glass bottles in Angolan supermarkets, the bulk of it is sold in small plastic sachets, like disposable ketchup wrappers. The men in this part of Angola call them 'Motorolas', because the sachets make it look like you are on the phone when you are drinking them while driving.

In the end, three men stepped forward and decided they would help us for a thousand kwanzas each. Sapalo was in his early twenties and like most people in the village, quite short for an adult, at about five feet four. He had a fantastic pair of bright-red three-quarter length shorts on, along with a Levi's t-shirt, white trucker hat and flip flops. His face was generally quite expressionless, with brown eyes and pronounced cheekbones. He was hardly dressed for an overland expedition, but he quickly stamped his authority on the adventure, swinging one of our dry bags onto his head and barking orders at two friends to pick up the remaining gear.

The first friend we think was called Yuri (he never introduced himself). One of the legacies of Soviet influence in Angola was that even out here in the rural areas, you would find people with Russian or Cuban-influenced names. Yuri was far more suitably dressed than Sapalo, with knee-length rubber boots, jean shorts and a stripy red-and-white t-shirt. He donned one of our lifejackets (which had served as back rests since about the second day of paddling) and also grabbed another dry bag. Our third assistant was Hélder. He was in his late teens and dressed in three-quarter-length jeans and a black tank top. Hélder seemed the friendliest, offering to carry bits of the kayak and laughing when we told him Guinness would not allow that!

As we set off down the path, one of Sapalo's younger cousins decided that he was coming along. He was about eight years old and hardly reached up to Alfy's waist. Hélder and Yuri smiled as the child buzzed around them, trying to grab gear so that he too could contribute to the hike (and get paid). In the end, he put on one of the lifejackets, which reached down to his knees, and grabbed a small green dry bag of electronics. As long as the adults were happy with him there, then so were we, and we set off on our merry way through the forest.

Figure 20 – Portage through the forests (19 June 2016)

Our 10km trek to the re-entry point took two and a half hours. Alfy had taken the much heavier section of the Klepper (the skin) whereas I had taken the more unwieldy bit (the wooden struts), which stuck out of the top of my hiking bag, adding an extra metre to my height as I smashed through the foliage. On a couple of occasions, I clotheslined myself while walking under a branch that I thought was low enough, but clearly was not.

Our journey was also slowed by the fact that Yuri kept having to stop and go to the toilet in the woods. We were beginning to see why he had not been enthusiastic about the whole enterprise; he was quite sick. Sapalo was not at all sympathetic, shouting at him to 'stop pooing so much' as we wound our way through the forest, much to the others' amusement.

Passing through one small village on our walk, the men were also busy getting drunk while the women were out in the fields. Other than that, we were alone. We arrived at the banks of the Kwanza, downstream but close enough to the rapids to hear them roaring in the distance. It was almost dark, so Sapalo and his crew were keen to head off home. We thanked them for their assistance, paid them and then they jogged back off into the forest.

Alone once again, Alfy and I fell back into our routine. Our first priority was to get the tents up. Then Alfy laid out the skin down by the river and set about reconstructing the Klepper by torchlight. I wandered out into the forest to gather firewood and begin preparing our food. If expeditions are made up of little victories, then there were few things as enjoyable as settling down for dinner after a hard day of exertion. Even the disgusting meals we were eating, usually a combination of rehydrated kidney beans, couscous and a foil-wrapped chorizo, tasted like *haute cuisine* after all that exertion. We discussed many issues around the campfire, but the main one was fantasising about all the different types of food and drink we would be able to savour once we reached Dando the following evening. For some reason, we were most excited by the prospect of hot, freshly baked bread.

That night I had one final job, which was to change the dressings on my feet. Walking along the trail, I could feel each foot getting worse and worse. I was concerned about what I would find underneath the gauze dressing. Peeling it back in my tent, things were just as bad as I had feared: the pads of both feet were covered by a single blister, about the size of a playing card, that stretched across the entire foot's width. They had even managed to make their way up the undersides of my big and little toes. Each one was filled with fluid, likely a combination of sweat and serum, but it was all pretty clear so no infection yet. The pain was intense. I drained and disinfected the whole area and patched it up as best I could, as I knew the following day would also involve some portage. My main concern was that my feet were going to be either wet in the kayak or being used for hiking for at least the next three weeks. When exactly were they going to get the chance to heal?

Monday, 20 June we were due to arrive in Dando, the town on the border between Bié and Malanje Provinces. The night before, I had tried to dry some wet clothing by placing it next to the fire. I woke up to find large holes burned into my paddling gloves, board shorts and one polo shirt. Still, the views made up for the minor inconvenience of damaged clothing.

The rapids that we had heard in the darkness overnight were only 100m upstream. There was a lone man stood on a rock in the middle of the rapids with a fishing rod. He shouted good morning to us and we waved back. It was impossible to see how he had hopped out there without a boat of some sort, but he seemed perfectly happy where he was. Another Kwanza mystery.

Alfy was looking dapper in his new khaki trousers, orange fleece and HALO woolly hat, making some final adjustments to the Klepper that he had been unable to do in the dark. Looking up at the shallow rapids behind us, I worried about the day ahead. We were going to have to navigate a lot of rough water between here and Malanje Bridge. I hoped our enthusiasm to get to Dando did not lead to a situation like the one we had faced in Camacupa.

It was an uneventful 12km of paddling before we hit the first major set of rapids. We unenthusiastically got out, dismantled the Klepper, loaded up all of our gear and began a 15km trek into Dando. My feet were burning with pain after only a few kilometres. The terrain was not particularly difficult, mainly mixed forest and farmland, providing plenty of shelter from the sun. Under other circumstances, this might even have been an enjoyable walk. But with each step, I could feel the fluid building up in my feet, like treading on a water balloon.

Eventually, the blisters had to burst, and they did, filling my Italian loafers with warm fluid that seeped in between my toes. To make matters worse, Dando played a cruel trick on us. The sun went down as we were approaching the town, and we could see lights up ahead in the distance, on the dirt road. We had almost arrived, thank goodness. In reality, we had to trek for another hour before reaching the centre of the settlement, where we could finally rest. The finish line was like a mirage in the desert, moving further and further away as we approached it.

Alfy and I headed for the largest building that was giving out the most light, assuming it would be the police station or the MPLA administrator's office – we probably needed to register at one or both of these upon arrival. Once we got there we were surprised to find that the building was, in fact, a private residence, running its own diesel generator, a very rare display of wealth in this rural area.

I was ready to collapse by this stage, my feet having gone

completely numb. There was a young boy sat on the porch of the house, reading a comic under the lightbulb.

'Where is the police station?' Alfy asked. Apparently it was further up the hill.

Before we could walk off, the door to the house burst open and out came Ali.

'Hello, my friends, what are you doing here? Please, sit, sit.'

Seeing the state I was in, Alfy offered to walk up the hill to find the police station, while I was more than happy to take Ali up on his offer.

'You must be very tired with such a large bag!' He whipped a 500 kwanza note out of his pocket and clicked his fingers at the boy. 'Go and fetch some cold drinks and some biscuits. Quickly.'

After a long day of drinking lukewarm filtered water, Ali's offer of cold drinks sounded great. Sitting down in the plastic lawn chair on the porch, all troubles melted away. In the light, I could now see that Ali was not Angolan, but Middle Eastern. He also spoke Portuguese with a strong accent, rolling many of his r's in a way that implied French was his preferred European language. After giving our standard spiel about who we were and what we were doing, I asked Ali what his story was.

'I am from Mauritania. I am here as a diamond trader.'

This was more great news. We immediately switched to speaking French, which was a lot less taxing on my stressed nervous system. The boy reappeared with a bag of cans of Coke and some chocolate biscuits. I practically inhaled the first can before realising I should probably have offered one to Ali.

'No, please, my friend, you need it more than me.'

We sat on the porch chatting for the next half an hour, during which time Ali's friend, a giant of a man called Nelson, appeared from the darkness and sat with us. They told me all about their work in Dando, buying diamonds directly from the *garimpeiros* who worked in the surrounding areas by the river. Ali was amazingly open, even giving me a short tour of his offices, which were basically two rooms, each with separate entrances. One had his desk and some filing cabinets.

'This is where we negotiate with the diamond sellers.'

The other was just a concrete floor with a mattress on it and a TV in the corner. Amazingly, he had a satellite dish on the building, and he turned the channel to France24. The news announcer was talking about the impending Brexit vote in the UK, while clips of David Cameron in the Houses of Parliament played.

'This is your country, yes? They are leaving the European Union?'

'No, Ali, we are soon voting on whether or not we wish to leave. But no decision has been made yet.'

'But this is a bad idea, *non*?'

'Oh yes, a very bad idea! But it should be OK. All of the polls suggest that the population of Britain will vote to remain in the EU.'

The whole thing was surreal: discussing Brexit with a Mauritanian diamond merchant in the Angolan bush. The vote was only three days away and I felt very far away from the action. Ali shook his head in disbelief. The idea of leaving the EU was incomprehensible to him. To many of his friends, the EU in general, and France in particular, was the promised land. It was where you went to get jobs, to look after your family, to live in safety. Ali told me that in his part of the world, the EU was a model of how things were supposed to work, of how nations were supposed to interact.

Having visited both France and Mauritania, I agreed with him on which nation was better governed. I was a little ashamed as the debate on France24 inevitably turned to immigration and the migrant crisis. The graphics on screen told us that Britain had taken in only a fraction of the number of refugees that other EU nations had. Again, Ali rolled his eyes and shook his head.

'*C'est triste.*'

I ate my biscuits, quietly nodding and wondering where Alfy was. A child came running down the hill with a message that I needed to follow him. I got up and looked around to say goodbye to Ali, but he had vanished into his office a few minutes earlier. Poking my head around the corner I was greeted by the stares of two shocked-looking men, sat across the table from Ali. Scattered across the table were a handful of medium-sized diamonds.

Ali stood up abruptly to say goodbye, ushering me outside away from the worried men, who he told me were Congolese. Ali even offered for us to crash in his office for the night, but I told him we already had lodgings and said goodbye, following the child up the hill into the darkness.

As in Soma Kuanza, it appeared that our reputation had preceded us. The HALO Trust team had already informed the local administration of our impending arrival and they had organised for us to stay with Dando's only doctor, in the health clinic opposite the police station. Alfy had pulled up a chair in the doctor's office and was watching the TV. I handed round the bag of soft drinks that Ali had sent me away with, and Alfy introduced me to the Angolan man whose clinic this must have been.

'Oscar, this is Guilherme. He says that Amadeu and Firmino spoke to him and arranged for us to sleep here tonight. Well, in the police station over the road anyway!'

Guilherme was bald and muscular with a big smile. He grabbed my hand with his huge paw and shook it vigorously. We all sat down in front of his grainy TV and watched some European football. There was a chart on one side of the cramped office with a diagram of the human body. A shelf held a few dusty medical textbooks but otherwise there was no hint that this was the only medical post for such a large settlement. Perhaps the drugs and equipment were stored elsewhere.

Noticing that I had limped into the room and proceeded to peel off my now rancid shoes, Guilherme took a look at my feet.

'This, you must clean. But do not worry, it is not a permanent injury. This will fix.'

I did not share his optimism, but before I could say a word, he had gone outside and reappeared with a plastic bucket filled with hot water. He placed it in front of me and I moved to put my feet in it. A foot bath seemed quite appealing at this stage.

'No, wait. We must add the disinfectant!'

Guilherme rummaged around in a nearby box and fished out a jar of what looked like salt crystals. He grabbed a generous handful and tossed them into the bucket, as if he were casting a spell over some sort of cauldron. Next, he found a lemon, cut it in half and crushed it in his powerful hand above the water, the juices and pips spilling out between his fingers and swirling in the bucket.

'Now, stir it and stick your feet in.'

One touch of the water and I realised it was way too hot to even put a finger in, let alone both my feet. Sensing my reticence, Guilherme reassured me.

'Hotter is better. Now get those feet in!'

He grabbed my feet and plunged them in. The pain was instant and excruciating. Salty, acidic, scalding water all over the raw skin. He held them in for what felt like an eternity, then I managed to pull them out, to much admonishment by Guilherme. Over the next hour I intermittently put my feet back in, slowly getting used to the feeling. Flexing my toes I could see all sorts of gunge floating up and sitting on top of the water: blood, pus, bits of my sock, even some gauze wrap from a few days ago. It did not feel good but it had to be doing something positive. All the while, I sat there, frustrated, staring at the screen.

'I don't think I can walk on these for all of tomorrow.'

According to our planned route, we would need to hike north-east out of Dando the next day, through the hills that led into the Luando Nature Reserve. The satellite photography showed it could be up to 40km before we reached a point in the river past the latest set of rapids where we could start paddling again.

Alfy was at a loss as to what to say. On reflection, I do not know what I expected him to say. There were only two options, and we both knew them: continue as planned, or stop now and admit defeat. Slowing down or taking a rest day, given all the delays up until this point, was also effectively admitting defeat, a point we had both agreed after my back issues at the beginning of the kayaking. My mind pored back over the decisions that had brought me to this point: was that 16km hike by the crash site worth it? Should I have found different shoes? Is there some magical drug in our medical kit that would sort this out?

'I know you don't want to hear this, but the problem you have is not a serious one. What I mean is, it's not like you have snapped a ligament in your knee. Mechanically, you are fine to walk. You're just going to have to find a way to deal with the pain.'

Alfy said what we were both thinking. It was a brutal reality check. I was desperate to come up with some solution, any, but could think of none. As I went to bed in a nearby police station bunk bed, my mind kept repeating a line from Cormac McCarthy's screenplay, *The Counselor*:

> *You are now at the crossing. And you want to choose, but there is no choosing there. There's only accepting. The choosing was done a long time ago.*

I had chosen to be here. I had told everybody we were going to succeed. Now I had to accept what success involved.

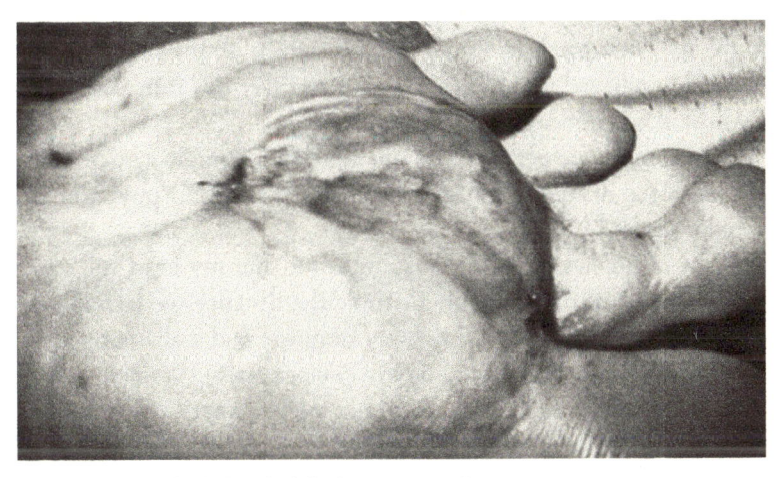

Figure 21 – My feet before the hike (21 June 2016)

The morning of Tuesday, 21 June began with the arrival of the HALO Trust Land Rover, complete with a resupply. Firmino was feeling a little better now, and they both expressed their regret for the state my feet were in. I strapped them up with as much tape as the medical kit could spare, popped a few codeine tablets and hoisted the weighty Klepper skeleton onto my back. Alfy did the same with the skin and we both set out, laden down with equipment. We had no idea what the path was like leading north, but many of the locals had said it was single track, so no room to assemble the buggy. These first 10km were hell.

The hills outside Dando are very steep and our route had us climbing up and down a number of them on cracked mud paths. My centre of gravity was high thanks to the Klepper struts sticking out of the top of my bag, making walking on a slope awkward. I was also trying my hardest to keep the soles of my feet flat, to avoid stretching out the pads and ripping open the dressings any further. We must have made quite a sight in the various villages we passed through on this section: Alfy, marching through with a determined stride, then me straggling behind, walking like a robot, with a bag of planks of wood pointing up at the sky. The combination of hills and my feet ground our average speed down to about 3kmph.

As I pulled myself up the most horrendous hill yet, I could see Alfy at the top, in a patch of shade. He was setting up the buggy. I was incredibly relieved at no longer having to carry this ridiculous load. By now it was midday and the sun was harsh.

'Listen, mate, we need to push on. We have a long way to go until we reach the diamond miner's village that the HALO guys said we could camp in.'

None of this was new information to me, but my heart still sank. We would need to do double or triple the distance we had already completed to stay on track. My body language said it all: slumped on the ground in the shade, avoiding eye contact, staring at my feet. Alfy and I were both raised in Britain, so not well equipped to express our emotions to one another. His frustration with our pace was etched all over his face. I was frustrated too. This foot problem seemed to be a black cloud hanging over the both of us. While screwing together the buggy, he said something I found truly touching.

'Forget about the 40km. You just need to do as much as you can manage and then we'll stop. Just try and get as far as possible. I'll drag the buggy and you walk. Just carry a water bottle and walk. I'll stop every 3km or so and wait for you and we can see how you're feeling.'

I could not believe he was offering to drag that 100kg+ buggy, on his own, across terrain that for all he knew was just as uneven as the

10km we had just finished. This was how much succeeding meant to Alfy. I felt ashamed of my weakness. I nodded in approval, thanked him, and we kept going in our new configuration; Alfy zooming up ahead like some sort of horse and cart and me hobbling behind with my water filtration bottle and a box of codeine tablets in my pocket.

Despite the extra weight, Alfy still made much faster progress than me. But he stopped, as promised, roughly every 3km. Thankfully, the terrain flattened out and we found ourselves walking through thick forest, which provided shelter from the sun. In certain sections, the baked-clay path was even quite dark. The foliage was dry and crackled as you brushed past it. This place had not seen rain for a while.

After another 9km, we got into a steady routine and the aim no longer seemed so insurmountable. I popped a few more codeine tablets to keep me going and trudged along, looking around at the forest for signs of wildlife but seeing very little besides small birds. On one occasion, I saw two black cat-like figures go scuttling off in my peripheral vision, perhaps mongoose or some type of hyrax.

Walking along, I could see Alfy's footsteps and the tyre marks from the cart in the dust in front of me. I followed them in a trance. Out of nowhere, I felt a wave of paranoia wash over me. Although he was stopping every 3km, Alfy was a long way ahead of me. I had no way of contacting him. I was alone. For some reason, I began to worry. First about the darkness of the forest and then about lions.

During the planning stage of the expedition, I had stumbled across a tale of lions from conservationist Pedro Vaz Pinto's 2013 expedition into the Luando Nature Reserve. Vaz Pinto is an Angolan biologist, credited with re-discovering the rare Angolan Giant Sable Antelope (*Palanca Negra*) in the wild in 2003, the first sighting in over 20 years. Many observers had feared that the *Palanca Negra* had gone extinct during the Angolan Civil War, prized for both its meat and its large curved horns, which can reach over 160cm. Pedro Vaz Pinto and a dedicated group of conservationists have worked hard over the past 15 years to bring these majestic creatures back from the brink of extinction.

These large beasts, who lend their name to the Angolan football team and their likeness to the national carrier TAAG, are still critically endangered. They only live in two places on earth: the Cangandala National Park, 40km south-east of Malanje, and just to the south, in the Luando Nature Reserve, into which Alfy and I were now trekking.

During a July 2013 capture operation, Pedro Vaz Pinto's team darted a large female *Palanca Negra*, in order to tranquilise her and fit a tracking collar. To their horror, as they hovered above in their helicopter waiting for the animal to collapse:

> ... a huge black-mane lion came out of nowhere, jumping from under the grass to the back of the female and quickly knocked her to the ground! We could not believe our eyes! There was a lion in Luando, and it had attacked a sable right underneath the chopper!

Luckily, they were able to scare away the lion before it did any damage to the immobilised *Palanca*, but it was confirmed: there were lions in the Luando Nature Reserve! In late 2014, Vaz Pinto reported that the lion attacked, killed and ate a poacher who had entered the reserve with a shotgun. The story was recounted by his terrified companion, who managed to flee the scene and seek help in a local village. In late 2015 the lion was confirmed to have killed and eaten a second poacher while he was checking his snares down by the Kwanza River. Again, the tale was recounted by the poacher's luckier accomplice who escaped.

Thinking logically, our chances of stumbling across this one man-eating lion in a park of 828 square kilometres were minuscule. But I was not thinking logically: I was sleep deprived, in pain and loaded up with far more codeine than was good for me. The next 10km of walking were performed at a faster pace, with a lot of scanning the treeline for movement. What would I do if I saw a lion anyway – climb a tree?

After a total of 25km of hiking, I hit the wall. Alfy was nowhere to be seen, it was late afternoon and all I wanted to do was get off my feet. I stumbled over to a shady area, sat down, leaned back against a tree trunk and closed my eyes. Just a few minutes of sleep could not hurt. My mind immediately raced back to Vaz Pinto's tales of the lion. This was not a good place to sleep. I stood up and marched on.

Figure 22   Male lion about to attack a tranquilised Palanca Negra in Luando Nature Reserve (2013). Image credit: Pedro Vaz Pinto

That day we covered 32km across rough terrain. For 22 of those kilometres, Alfy dragged the buggy on his own, never once complaining. We arrived in the village of Sacangala after dark and spoke to the village *soba* who said we were welcome to camp anywhere, or even sleep in one of the huts. Our bedroom for the night was a mud-brick storage building in the centre of the village, filled with a leaking motorbike, a diesel generator and some dirty mattresses. It still beat setting up our tents in the dark.

We laid out our sleeping bags on the floor and were keen to go straight to sleep, but the children in the village had other ideas. One by one, ten of them barged into the small building and took up perches on a bench, staring at us. The leader of the pack, barely seven years old, introduced himself as Alfredo. We asked who the other children were.

'These are my brothers.'

'So you all have the same mother?'

'No, no, no. But we have the same father!'

I got out the video camera and began to film them, flipping the screen so that they could see what was being recorded. For some strange reason this prompted Alfredo and his brothers to start dancing wildly. Exhausted as we were, it was good to end the hike with an evening dance party.

As expected after so much hiking, I woke on Wednesday, 22 June to throbbing pain in my feet. Both pads were swollen, raw and infected. There were a variety of coloured liquids seeping from them into my sleeping bag and none of them smelled particularly pleasant. My usual routine of draining, disinfecting and bandaging began, in the hope that we did not have too much of a hike before we got back in the Kwanza. Alfy's feet were also suffering by this stage, and as he peeled off his socks that morning, he took a fair amount of skin with them. We both needed to get our feet out of their boots and into the sun on the river.

It was only a 4km walk out of the village to a point where we could re-enter the Kwanza. Just outside our hut, an old lady was pounding cassava into flour using a wooden pole, while pigs and chickens fussed around her. An MPLA flag fluttered in the wind. As always, it was chilly this morning. As soon as we exited the village, we passed a group of diamond miners. A diver had just come out of the water and was showing his friends his latest haul of silt from the river bed. They waved us over, then offered to show us a good entry point, but not before they had tried their hardest to sell us some diamonds.

One of them reached into his pocket and pulled out a folded piece of paper. Inside was a collection of small translucent stones. I have no idea of the quality of the stones he showed us, or if they were even diamonds, but they assured us that this section of the river provided particularly rich pickings. As always, we politely declined.

Our re-entry point was a white sand beach, which was perfect for assembling the Klepper. Quite an audience gathered as we assembled her, all of them arguing about what the finished product was going to look like and how the various pieces would fit together. The foot-peddle-controlled rudder was very impressive, as was our solar panel.

'This is for controlling the engine. It is the accelerator!' said one bystander, pointing to the rudder pedals.

'No, you fool, there is no engine.' Judging by the tone, this was probably his wife.

We wanted to cover at least 50km of paddling, and the day started well. The river was wide, fast flowing and clear of any major obstacles. According to Alfy's satellite photography, there were no waterfalls or rapids today. Thirty-five kilometres into the day though, at about 4pm, we hit another obstacle that would stop us in our tracks and force an early camp.

We were paddling along a long, straight section when we noticed two objects floating in the water up ahead, 300m in the distance. We thought little of it at first, as we would often see debris being swept along such as logs or floating river weed. However, these two objects were not floating along with the current, they were stationary. Could they be rocks? At about 200m we decided that rocks were the most likely explanation and decided to head through the middle of them, given their adequate spacing. Having committed to this course of action, at 150m out, we suddenly heard an urgent cry from one of the trees.

'Do you have rifles?'

This seemed like an odd question to open with. Scanning the banks, we saw a man stood on an overhanging tree branch, waving to get our attention.

'No, no rifles. Why?' I responded, confused.

'Because those hippos kill!'

We looked downriver again, and, sure enough, those were the heads of two large male hippos, not rocks. The tell-tale silhouette of their nostrils and eyes poking above the waterline gave them away, once we knew what to look for. Huge beasts, almost completely submerged. Watching us.

Their behaviour was unusual. Most of the previous hippos would have dived underwater and vanished by now, given the noise we were making. But these two were just sat there, staring, directly in our path. We paddled backwards to slow our progress as we spoke to the fisherman.

'What do you mean they kill? They will attack this boat?'

'Oh yes. That guy and his two sons. They are very aggressive. Very dangerous!'

Beyond these alarmist comments, the man was vague. We wanted to know if he had any personal experience of these specific hippos attacking people or if he was making a more general comment on the dangerous unpredictability of hippos. It was very difficult to get a straight answer. We offered to pay the fisherman to show us a safe path around the hippos. He refused, regardless of the amount offered.

This lack of clarity meant different things to Alfy and me. To me, it was an indication that we should get out and seek advice at the man's village. To Alfy, it meant we should push on and see what happened. In the end, we went for the latter approach, with me creeping along the river bank, ready to haul the kayak out of the water and Alfy slowly floating it down the river along the treeline, keeping an eye on the hippos. Sure enough, the closer we got, the more noise the hippos made and the closer they swam towards the Klepper. Their deep laughter and occasional exhales echoed across the water. They were deliberately obstructing our path. With the three hippos less than 50m away, we retreated back to the village to camp for the night, disappointed at the early finish and yet another delay.

The village *soba* told us many tales of how these hippos had been terrorising the residents for years, upending fishing boats, chasing people collecting water and making it unsafe to navigate the river at certain times of day. Everyone knew that it was a father and his two sons but, disappointingly, they did not have names. The whole community had adjusted their fishing and travel schedule as a result of these animals. We were amazed that in all this time nobody had got hold of a rifle and shot them, given the availability of weapons in rural Angola.

The *soba* said that early the following morning we would be escorted past the hippos by two fishermen. The nominated fishermen were less than enthusiastic about this duty but nodded solemnly in acquiescence.

Thursday, 23 June was a tense day for a number of reasons. We were due to run the hippo gauntlet while back home our fellow countrymen were busy voting in a referendum to decide whether or not Britain should remain in the European Union. Our fishermen escorts asked us if we were willing to wait until that afternoon, when the hippos tended to head further upriver to graze. We said that we could not wait that long. The men explained the plan which was basically: sneak up the right-hand bank, pulling ourselves along the overhanging tree branches as quietly as possible. This was the same plan that had not worked the afternoon before, but they reassured us.

'What do we do if the hippos come over?'

'Get out of your kayak and into the trees… quickly!'

Great. The plan, assuming they attacked, was essentially to abandon our Klepper and all of our gear to the whims of three angry hippos. We crossed our fingers and set off into the morning mist, towards the grunts.

The two fishermen were in front, in a battered two-man dugout canoe. One man was at the front, sat down and paddling, and one at the back, stood up and punting. The whole back section of their canoe was broken and barely above the waterline, as if it had been bitten. We did not ask about it. The moon was still visible in the early morning sky. There were sections of overhanging tree that offered safety, if we could get up them in time. These were interspersed with sections of tall grass on steep banks that would be very difficult to scale in an emergency.

Sure enough, two hippo heads emerged from the water and began grunting aggressively. They were on the other side of the river, so we pushed on. They vanished underwater, then reappeared 20 seconds later in the centre of the river, with a loud exhale of breath that startled us all. They were heading straight for us.

The lead male charged along the surface at incredible speed for such a heavy creature. The fishermen screamed at us to get out, and we turned our backs to the impending threat, ramming the kayak into the treeline on the right bank, the hippos now within 30m of us. All four of us scrambled up into the branches, looking down at our stranded vessels. If the hippos sank the boats, we were well and truly stuck.

The hippos paused, facing upriver and swimming to maintain a stationary position relative to us on the bank. Perhaps they have poor eyesight and could no longer see us? Whatever the reason they halted their advance, we were thankful, but they were not retreating. They were just floating there, flicking their ears and occasionally grunting. We needed them to move upriver or back over to the other side of the water. If they allowed themselves to be carried downriver, we could have to do this whole thing again.

Figure 23 – An aggressive male hippo keeps a close eye on us (23 June 2016)

After 15 minutes the hippos lost interest and swam off upriver, towards the terrorised village. When they were 100m away, we snuck back into our kayak and paddled as hard as we could until we were at least 500m from the scene. We then thanked the fishermen, paid them for their time and headed on. They told us that they were going to park their dugout nearby and trek back up to the village. This sounded like a sensible move to us.

We only managed three hours of calm paddling before hitting another obstacle: more diamond mines. The river narrowed down from over 200m wide to less than 100m, becoming much more shallow; perfect conditions for mining. The first indication that this set of mines would be different to the ones we had seen previously was the sound of construction vehicles and the plumes of dust being kicked up by all the excavation works.

As we paddled along, we could see both Angolan and Chinese drivers of heavy plant equipment occasionally coming close to the bank as they cleared trees and scrubland to make room for construction. The noise meant we could not get their attention and they were unlikely to look out onto the river anyway. Boats did not come down into these areas very frequently.

Eventually we reached a point on the map where Alfy had calculated we needed to get out and portage around rapids. These were the feature that had attracted the miners. We spent the next 10km getting in and out of the river, slowly working our way past the obstacles. Every time we got out, we saw signs of human activity: bulldozed pathways through the bush, litter, burned sections of grassland. We even saw some chain-link fencing. The tyre tracks on the road that ran parallel to the river were fresh, but there was nobody in sight on this section. We could hear their engines, working in the distance.

We found a Chinese heavy goods vehicle abandoned by the side of the road. I climbed up into the cab, which was open, but there were no keys. Perhaps it had broken down. On one section of trekking across this post-apocalyptic landscape, we almost got lost due to the proliferation of trails. The damage that had been wrought on the environment was shocking. Even more so as we were right on the edge of the Luando Nature Reserve. Admittedly, all of the construction work had occurred on the west bank of the river, technically outside the reserve, but this level of destruction had to affect the ecosystem just over the water. Who knew what was being dumped into the river. We ended the day dejected at only having covered 35km and camped by the side of one of these bush roads.

Friday, 24 June was the day of the referendum result in the UK: were we staying in the European Union or leaving? As we were packing up our camp and getting ready to start paddling, a Toyota Land Cruiser came speeding down the dirt track in a cloud of dust. They came within ten metres of our tents, but did not slow down, skidding around some trees and off into the bush. Then we heard their brakes slamming on and the sound of reverse gear engaged. The driver had spotted us. This was not necessarily good news, as the 4×4 had the logo of a private security company on the side, and they tended to carry weapons. Alfy and I were also unsure as to how happy they would be having foreigners on their concession.

The four armed men wound down their windows, did a double-take and said good morning. One of them laughed when we said we had paddled from Soma Kuanza. It was impossible, he declared. They told us that the mining activity continued downriver for many kilometres, but that we should be clear to paddle for a few days up ahead. This was music to our ears as we set off.

That day we set an expedition record for distance covered: 63km in total. During this time, we avoided three lone hippos and also smashed the Klepper over a set of rapids that it would have been wiser to portage around. Following on from the sinking, we had been taking a much more cautious approach to rapids. One of us would get out, hike ahead and recce the route, either through the rapids or around them. On this occasion, it was Alfy's turn to get out and figure out a route. Meanwhile, I parked up at the side of the river and watched the miners on the other side.

They had a large metal cable across the river, which they had attached their dredging pontoon to. Some men were busily at work in the centre of the river, while others were filtering sediment on the other bank. They had burned all the grassland to make room for their blue tarpaulin tents. Some 4x4s were parked up under the trees and a large white flag signalled their position to any passing river traffic. I could see two satellite dishes and at least a hundred men. This was a serious operation.

Alfy returned and said there was a route through the central section of rapids that were roaring up ahead. I had long since learned to ignore the sound the rapids made, as they seemed to provide no reliable indication of ferocity. Wherever the river was wide, the rapids sounded terrifying, regardless of strength. With this in mind, we shunted off and paddled hard downriver.

We dropped down the first few shelves without a problem. The miners on the other bank stopped what they were doing and lined up by the river, shouting encouragement to us. Then we went flying over a much steeper ledge. The nose pointed down and as the front paddler I was staring directly into the river. There was no time to think about what a bad idea this drop was before we went over.

As we splashed down, we managed to get the kayak wedged perpendicular to the current in a shallow section. A recipe for another sinking. We quickly jumped out, to find we were only in knee-high water. The miners loved this and gave us a loud cheer, laughing as we pushed ourselves out of the rapids, without taking on too much water.

Alfy and I had a few words after that as to what type of rapids were suitable for kayaking and what type needed to be portaged around!

Despite this near miss, we managed to cover a lot of distance that day with no other incidents. Apart from the usual talk of rapids, hippos and diamond mines, we spent most of the afternoon discussing the UK referendum. My brother had agreed to text us the result that evening on the satellite phone, which was an exciting intrusion from the outside world. This was such a significant event in UK political history, it felt strange being so far removed from it. But I had given my girlfriend my vote by proxy. Now I just had to hope Steph had used it wisely. Alfy and I spent a few hours arguing as to whether EU membership was a positive or negative thing for the UK. Alfy leaned vaguely towards Brexit. I was a pretty adamant Remainer. In the end we had to agree to disagree.

Our political debate was interrupted by the appearance of another mine. Alfy had marked some potential rapids on the map up ahead, so we moored at their jetty and walked onto the land. This group had a boat with an outboard motor and we could see a new dirt bike leaning against a tree by the makeshift tarpaulin shelters. This was not the usual Chinese knock-off but a well-maintained white-and-red KLM bike, an unusual sight in these parts. Up ahead of us there was a temporary hut, constructed of logs and corrugated iron. From the delicious smells in the air, it seemed that we had arrived at a meal time.

Would you like to buy some diamonds?

Walking up to the hut, we saw fish being barbecued over hot coals and generous plates of *funge* with a thick sauce poured over them. It was mouth-watering. The chef, a short Angolan man stooped over a steaming pot, greeted us in a nonchalant manner and asked how he could help, eventually calling over the camp supervisor.

A tall, muscular-framed bald man in smart shoes, clean jeans and a collared shirt came striding over confidently. As he shook our hands vigorously, we noted a fancy gold watch on his wrist.

'Welcome to the camp. My name is Jean-Claude. Where are you from?'

'We are British. We have kayaked all the way here from Soma Kuanza in that.' Alfy pointed to the battered Klepper.

There was uproar from the chef and a couple of the hungry miners waiting for their food. 'It cannot be!' 'That's so far away!' The usual response. Jean-Claude simply whistled quietly.

'It's great to meet you. Where are you from?' Alfy continued. His distinctive accent and name told us he was not Angolan. Our first guess was Congolese, but it was not a good idea to ask this directly. The two countries have a very troubled shared history, which continues to cause problems for Congolese migrants in Angola to this day.

'I am from Central Africa.'

Jean-Claude smiled politely. We did not push the issue, but it was clear he did not mean the Central African Republic. I suggested that we switch to French for ease of communication. He agreed and invited us to sit on some plastic chairs in front of the canteen and we happily obliged. The chef even offered us a plate of food, but we declined, not wanting to deprive the camp of supplies. I really wish we had said yes, as it smelled delicious.

'So how long have you been out here? Who do you work for?'

Again, I had to be very careful about my line of questioning, recalling the warnings we received back in Luanda. The miners on this section of the Kwanza are secretive for a reason: a lot of the mines operate in a grey legal space and some are outright illegal, with no permission at all from central government.

'I have been working in this area since the 1980s. We first came out here as part of a cooperation deal between the Angolan government and the former government of Zaire, under Mobutu. Back then we worked with Gécamines, although now this is not the case. Now, we work for ourselves.'

Jean-Claude said that they had been in their current location for a few months and were doing quite well in terms of their diamond haul. Looking back at the tattered tents, I asked him when the last time he went home was.

'I have not been back to see my family for ten weeks. But this is normal for us. When one searches for lucre, one has to be willing to tolerate a certain level of discomfort.'

His French was impeccable and he demonstrated a rich vocabulary. It is hard to remember the last time I heard anyone use the term 'lucre' in English, but in French it was the perfect fit for the context: this really was dishonourable wealth that they were plundering from the Kwanza's bed.

Jean-Claude was clearly a well-educated man and keen to talk about the problems 'foreign' workers faced in this industry while in Angola. He of course meant Congolese.

'There is no work over the border. Many come here to provide for their families. Or they are brought here by Angolan companies that then do not provide them with work permits or any protection if the security forces pick them up. Some of us have been here for so long, this place becomes home for us. But we have no papers, no rights. You see what happens in the other areas, in Lunda-Norte and Lunda-Sul.'

Jean-Claude was referring to the recent mass-expulsion of artisan Congolese miners on the Angolan side of the border up in the northeast of the country. These unfortunate workers were historically used as pawns in the volatile relations between the governments in Luanda and Kinshasa. Populist Angolan politicians also knew that stirring up anti-Congolese sentiment with a few xenophobic remarks to the press was great for boosting their profile. In 2011, the United Nations

Would you like to buy some diamonds?

Office for the Coordination of Humanitarian Affairs (UNOCHA) documented over 100,000 Congolese expulsions in a particularly bad year.

As with many areas in Africa where high-value natural resources are up for grabs, reports of human rights abuses were commonplace. In May 2015, Angolan investigative journalist Rafael Marques was handed a six-month suspended jail term for defaming Angolan military leaders in his 2011 book *Blood Diamonds: Corruption and Torture in Angola*. The book detailed serious human rights abuses in the Lunda provinces by private security companies guarding the diamond mines, including torture, rape and murder. It was these sorts of stories that had coloured our initial attitude towards the diamond mining projects on the Kwanza: steer well clear. However, we could see no evidence of these kinds of abuses here.

'Here, security is not such a problem. We are much more isolated and far from the border. There is no concern that the diamonds will be stolen.'

We were happy that was the case. Dodging trigger-happy security contractors every time we passed a mine would have made the journey borderline impossible.

After buying up the canteen's supply of cold drinks (which consisted of six cans of Blue Orange), we said our goodbyes and continued paddling. That evening, we had to haul all of our gear up a sheer slope in order to camp in a forest at the end of our 63km paddle. We camped on the right-hand bank of the river, still within the Luando Nature Reserve.

The whole area had recently been burned, meaning that only large trees had survived. The rest of the ground was blackened and cleared, although there were a few glowing embers still around. At the time we were not worried about fire sweeping back through this area as there was little left to burn. On reflection, this was probably not the safest place to camp. Five hundred metres further inland, we could hear the sound of the fire still burning and, occasionally, even see the flames in the evening light. It had seemed like a great spot to camp: no insects, no long grass for snakes to hide in, plus plenty of dried out logs for our fire.

That evening, as we sat around the fire discussing plans for the next day, a hippo surfaced down at the water's edge and walked out onto the bank, about 20m from our camp. He was hard to see in all the undergrowth, but we could certainly hear him, crashing around in the thicket and grunting loudly. The only route up to where we were sitting was via the very steep bank: we had only been able to scale it by crawling on our hands and knees, grabbing hold of tree roots for leverage. We assumed this was an insurmountable obstacle for the heavy hippo. Just in case, we stoked the fire larger and shouted at him to go away. He got the message, slipping back into the water, grunting his disapproval as he went.

Over dinner, we switched on the satellite phone and waited for the text message from my brother about the referendum result. Most of the polls before I had left Britain for Angola predicted an easy victory for the Remain camp. Even Alfy was expecting a clear vote in favour of remaining in the European Union. My brother's short message hit hard:

'We're leaving the EU.'

What an incredible turn of events. The British public had voted by 51.89 per cent to 48.11 per cent to leave. We were both shocked. Alfy was the first to speak.

'Wow. Even I wasn't expecting that. That's unbelievable. I wonder how many of the Leave campaigners actually thought they would win?'

'Not that many, I imagine! Boris Johnson has a big mess to clean up now. Why on earth would anyone vote for something so damaging to the UK's interests?'

'Well, I never registered to vote by proxy. But I know my dad said he was going to vote Leave. I believe the short-term economic issues are worth going through for the flexibility that independence from the EU will afford us to run our economy the way we want. We were never going to be able to effect reform from the inside.'

'I just don't understand. I guess being half-Italian I'm more inclined to side with the continent on this, but the EU has brought so many positives. Single market membership? Customs union? I am baffled that we would be willing to throw access to those things away.'

'We'll have to see. Tell your brother to send us more updates. I want to know how David Cameron is going to react!'

Alfy and I talked late into the night, which was unusual given how tired we both always were. This was one of the few times where we both wished for an internet connection, or access to a TV. What were our friends saying about this back home? What about the politicians? How were the markets reacting? We had never felt more isolated from the outside world.

The morning of Saturday, 25 June was another tense, early start. All thoughts of Brexit were set aside. We had a more pressing concern: was that a hippo lurking out there and, if so, did he begrudge us camping on his patch? As we set out in the early-morning light, the extent of the fire damage on the right-hand side of the river became apparent: it stretched for kilometres. Later in the morning, we saw that it also spread across both sides of the river. We paddled through a still smoking, blackened wasteland for hundreds of metres at a time.

This did not seem to have put the hippos off; they were out in abundance. On three separate occasions, we had to sprint the width of the river to avoid large pods blocking our path. Following the issues with the aggressive males a few days earlier, we were even more cautious and gave them a very wide berth, which was easier now that the river had opened out.

Forty-five kilometres into our day of paddling, we came across a large diamond mine on the west bank of the Kwanza, which stretched 2km along the river. We shouted our usual greetings to the confused-looking miners on the other side of the water and asked if they had anything to sell us.

'Why don't you come and look in the shop?' one of them yelled back.

Alfy and I could not believe our ears. A shop? We raced over to the other side and moored the Klepper. It turned out that due to the size of the mining community in this camp, there were actually two shops, both garden shed-like arrangements with a locking door and even awnings to keep browsing customers out of the sun!

Alfy walked over to one while I had a look at the other. We reconvened five minutes later with our haul: canned Portuguese sardines in spicy tomato sauce. Chupa Chups lolly pops. Fizzy drinks. Powdered hot chocolate. Weird salty biscuits. They even sold us a can of Cuca beer each, for only six times the street price in Luanda (three hundred kwanzas each). It was a banquet as far as we were concerned.

The last 15km of the day were a breeze, as we raced along on a sugar high. That evening, we found a series of mud steps carved into the high bank, presumably by a fishing party. While cutting across the river to finish for the evening, we had one final incident when a lone hippo surfaced out of nowhere to see what we were doing, giving us quite a shock. As quickly as he had arrived, he left again.

We quickly moored, climbed up the steps and onto a plateau overlooking the river, dotted with termite nests. The fishermen's fire was still smouldering from the night before. As we sipped our Cuca and looked out over the water, the next phase of our expedition was almost in sight. If all went well the following day, we would reach the Malanje Bridge and a promised resupply from the HALO Trust. Then it should only be three more days until we reached Capanda Dam. We were both excited about the dam for the same reasons: not only did it represent the point of having completed two-thirds of the expedition. It also meant entering a far more predictable (and safe) section of the expedition: no more hippos, much more accurate mapping of rapids and closer population centres if help was required. Alfy and his brothers had even kayaked this last third already, which further reassured us that it was doable. The end was almost in sight.

On Sunday, 26 June we woke up exactly 60km south of Malanje Bridge. The river was 250m wide and we knew there were hippos around as we had seen one, and several of them had disturbed our sleep the previous evening with their loud grunting and splashing. It only took half an hour for us to see our first set of hippos. After a brief glimpse of their fat rear ends wobbling on the bank, they all went crashing into the water as soon as they heard us. There were at least three, all vanishing underwater rapidly, then reappearing worryingly far away from their submersion points a few seconds later. After pausing to assess, we sprinted across to the other side of the river and continued cautiously along the left bank.

Much of the morning was taken up with negotiating light rapids and fighting against a strong headwind. Just before lunchtime, we approached a massive set of rapids, over 500m wide, on a sweeping meander. These were the *sete ilhas* rapids that Alexandre had warned us about in Camacupa. We had the choice of barrelling straight through, cutting out the meander but braving the worst of the white water, or creeping along the meander, with no idea what exactly would be waiting for us around the blind corner.

After seeking advice from a local fisherman, we opted for the corner and were rewarded with a terrifying 2km ordeal of rapids interspersed with sand banks. The battered Klepper held up remarkably well, although we did end up scraping her over some rocks in sections, threatening to pierce the already worn skin.

The river kept us on our toes all afternoon, with a series of rapids, often around islands in the river. The benefit of this section was that the current added to our average speed, making up for the headwind and sweeping us along towards Malanje Bridge. The landscape became greener as we approached the settlement and for the first time palm trees and other tropical plants started to dot the skyline on each bank. We even saw some large farms using the Kwanza for irrigation.

Alfy had noted a large waterfall a few kilometres before the bridge, known as Porto Condo, so we were on alert as we steamed down the rapids. In a rare break between white water, a farmer on the side of the river started shouting to us.

'You! You need to get out! Up ahead it's dangerous! You cannot take your boat down there!'

Alfy shouted back to reassure him we would be getting out before the waterfall.

'No! You must get out now! This is the last place you can get out!'

According to our map he was wrong. We had another 3km to go before we needed to portage around the waterfall. We paused, paddling backwards to stay still, while Alfy checked the GPS trail. Local knowledge had already proven invaluable more than once. We did not want to take a risk on an obstacle as serious as this one. The man kept screaming for us to get out, as if his life depended on it. It was really disconcerting.

No. Alfy was confident. The man was wrong. We shouted thanks to him and paddled on cautiously.

'You're doomed! You will die!'

His warnings soon faded into the distance, drowned out by the sound of a lot of white water.

The Porto Condo waterfall was easy to hear and easy to spot. The spray from the drop shot up into the late-afternoon air and the sound was unmistakable. The waters leading up to the falls were very calm, so we were able to paddle right up to the edge. Here we surprised various groups of Angolan tourists, mainly day-trippers from nearby Malanje, the provincial capital 35km to the north. There were quite a few people, paddling around near the edge or taking selfies with the sunset behind them.

We unpacked our gear, stuck the Klepper on our shoulders and then carried it along the path that led from the top of the waterfall to the calm waters beyond it. This seemed to be a popular weekend spot for young Angolans to congregate: there was a bar, a dirt football pitch and a large space for car parking. Some people were even swimming at the foot of the falls. We paused for a while to chat to people and ask about obstacles further up. The men in fibreglass boats, running a water taxi service, told us that there were few hippos up ahead but gave us the rough locations of the main rapids they knew of. Our goal was in sight, just 3km further down the river, with the sun setting behind it. We had made it to Malanje Bridge!

We were half expecting to see the HALO Trust Land Rover parked up on the bridge, looking out for us, but they were nowhere to be seen. There was, however, an Angolan couple, taking photos and waving down to us. Gerhard's advice had been to avoid the foot of bridges because of the mine risk, but we had little choice when choosing an exit point from the river. The rest of the bank was thick reeds and bog. We chose a well-worn path on the east bank and moored.

A hundred metres up the hill, by the road entry point to the bridge, was a bright-blue hut. This was a police checkpoint. The bridge itself was two lanes wide, with solar-powered lighting along both approach roads. The archways underneath gave it a distinctive profile against the backdrop of the setting sun. On the side that we had landed, there

Figure 24 – Passing the waterfall at Porto Condo (26 June 2016)

was a wrecked Soviet tank in the undergrowth. Another one sat in the bush on the other side of the approach road, covered in white graffiti.

We had now left the Luando Nature Reserve, whose western border was demarcated by the course of the Kwanza River. It was time to turn westwards and start paddling directly towards the ocean. Thirty kilometres to our east, oddly separated from the Luando Nature Reserve, was the smallest national park in Angola: the Cangandala National Park. Founded in 1963, this is the only other location in the world to host populations of *Palanca Negra*. It was a shame not to be able to pause and take this opportunity to explore this remote wilderness, but we were on a tight schedule.

We walked up to the *Posto De Polícia* to register our presence in this new province and ask if the HALO Trust vehicle had arrived. We had now left Bié Province and entered Malanje Province. A cheerful young policeman called Oscar came out to greet us, his official blue uniform covered by a thick coat, scarf and hat, as if he was heading off up a mountain. He loved that I had the same name and immediately welcomed us into his police hut.

'We have seen no one from the HALO Trust, but you can wait for them here. First, you need to speak to my boss. I will take you.'

With that, we left the Klepper outside the police building and were loaded onto his spluttering Chinese motorbike (Keweseki, not Kawasaki) for a trip to the main police station a kilometre down the road from the bridge. Here, we were introduced to the gruff and unfriendly Comandante Paulo. He was short, overweight and not particularly welcoming.

'Where are your papers?' he barked in an accusatory tone. 'Where are your passports?'

We handed over a few stacks of tattered paperwork from Alfy's bag, including all the permits he had secured from the various ministries. Luckily, all of this documentation had been in waterproof pouches during the sinking and remained legible.

Comandante Paulo grunted in vague approval. We sat outside his office, chatting to Oscar while the commander got on his mobile phone and called his superiors.

'We have two British here... tourists... No, they came here on the river... No, the river... They are saying they wish to continue and they have permissions...'

The line was bad and he was shouting. We could hear every word from outside on the chairs. It did not sound good.

Comandante Paulo walked back out of his office. 'You should have arranged your arrival before you got here. We were not expecting you. We do not have the facilities to verify your documentation here. You will need to go to Malanje and do it.'

We reassured the commander that all of our paperwork was in order and that a 70km round trip to Malanje was not necessary.

'Our friends from the HALO Trust will be here soon. They can confirm to you what we are doing.'

Comandante Paulo warmed to us a little after we mentioned the HALO Trust. Everyone in this part of the country knew who they were, or had a friend or relative positively impacted by their mine clearance work in neighbouring provinces, although most of the demining in Malanje Province is handled by Norwegian People's Aid (NPA), which has been present in Angola since the 1990s. He sifted through the paperwork in his hand then smiled at us.

'OK, you can camp here tonight, while we sort out the paperwork. In the morning, you can continue your journey.'

That night we cooked up our dinner in the police hut down by the bridge. The HALO Trust Land Rover was nowhere to be seen. After texting Gerhard on the satellite phone, we were told that there had been a logistics mix up and that Amadeu and Firmino were not coming.

This was a serious problem, as no vehicle meant no ration resupply. One hasty motorbike trip later, we were loaded up with locally bought supplies including suspicious chorizos with no expiry date on them and some 'Super Maria' chocolate biscuits that did not look very super. Beyond selling copious quantities of cheap alcohol, none of the shops in town had much nutritious food we could purchase.

After our shopping trip we returned to the police hut. At 8pm, Oscar was joined by his friend Elias, who was also on the night shift. Elias was much older, definitely of the generation that had lived through the civil war. I asked him how much this area had changed since 2002, pointing to the new bridge.

'Here we have very good development. You see we have the road which is strong, we have the bridge to Cangandala and Malanje. You can easily reach Malanje and there we have an airport. If you want, you can drive all the way to Luanda from here. During the war, all of this was impossible. FAPLA and the Cubans, they were all around here in 1986, guarding the cities against UNITA. Travel between settlements was very difficult. Checkpoints everywhere. Many bandits.'

I asked him what his job was on the night shift.

'We are here to control the traffic. We must protect against bandits.'

There seemed to be a lack of both traffic and bandits that night.

To pass the time, Oscar and Elias cranked up the radio to full volume, filling the night air with blasting *kizomba* tunes. They then proceeded to shout a conversation at each other for the whole night. That night the air was thick with mosquitos. We wished we had camped by the river.

On Monday, 27 June, back up the road at the main police station, we said goodbye to Comandante Paulo and ensured that he was happy with our paperwork. His attitude towards us had improved considerably overnight. He shook our hands, asked a few questions about the problems we expected to face on the remaining journey and how long it would take us to get back to Luanda. The commander was sceptical as to whether we would finish, but wished us all the best as we loaded up and set off again. Our next target was Capanda Dam, two days' paddling to the north-west. It was at this point that we would have to get out and portage around the hydroelectric installations and rapids.

It was a tough day of paddling, with a lot of difficult choices about which route to take. The river kept splitting into separate channels and there were numerous sections with islands and sand banks dividing the main course. Without the GPS device and Alfy's careful route planning, we would have been hopelessly lost. Once again, we went flying down a steep drop on the water due to poor choice of line, but no lasting damage was done to the kayak.

The landscape continued to become greener along this section and the heat was intense. The river ballooned out to 1.2km wide in parts. This was ancient forest, with tropical vines and trees jutting out from every available piece of land. Such landscape was worrying as it made portage impossible and would also make it extremely difficult if we needed to bail out in an emergency.

That afternoon, while paddling between two jungle-covered islands in the centre of the river, we startled a hippo who was grazing at the top of a steep bank. Upon seeing us approaching, he threw himself off the bank, dropping three metres through the air and belly-flopping into the river. He was obscured by reeds, so we never got a good look at him, but based on the waves he generated he must have been a mature adult male. We sprinted through that section, keenly aware that he may have been chasing us, rather than running away.

Beyond this brief bit of hippo excitement, we were always listening for the tell-tale sounds of rapids. It was good fun pausing in front of them, selecting a route, then committing to the drop. Three or four times we got wedged on rocks and had to dive into the water to guide the Klepper to safety. Every time this happened, the skin of the kayak was worn down further. How long would it be before we felt water seeping in around our bare feet?

By 5.30pm we were both exhausted. The fast-flowing water had helped us set another expedition record, as we broke the 70km barrier that day. By chance, while stopping to ask some fishermen about a decent spot to camp, they directed us to their village, right near the bank but completely obscured by foliage. They chuckled as they pointed around the corner: had we continued another 500m, we would have shot off the end of a small waterfall.

We set up camp by the water, swatting away the numerous bloodsucking insects that were loitering in the twilight air. A few of the villagers came down and told us we were OK to camp there, but would need to move briefly as some of the women wanted to bathe at the foot of the waterfall. We politely averted our eyes while they did this and then tried to wash as quickly as possible while mosquitoes feasted on every bare bit of flesh they could land on. It was a relief to get our clothes back on.

That night, as Alfy and I sat around the fire, an old man came ambling along the river, with a home-made fishing rod slung over his shoulder.

'Do you boys have any fish?' he slurred. He appeared to have been drinking heavily.

'No, sorry. We only have the food we brought with us.'

'Oh no. My wife is going to kill me! I was supposed to catch fish for dinner, but there are no fish.'

He waded into the water, splashing everywhere and cast his line. The line was only a metre long and had no hook or bait on the end. After 30 seconds he pulled it out and was genuinely frustrated that a fish had not somehow entangled itself.

'She will kill me,' he muttered, stumbling off towards the village.

By Tuesday, 28 June we were only 70km east of Capanda Dam. If we got a good day in, we could be camping at our destination that evening, ready to clip together the buggy and get hiking. The day began wending our way through a maze of islands, mini-rapids and dense vegetation. There were more scrapes across the hull that had us holding our breath, waiting for the water to rush in.

All morning the river continued to be wide, around 500m and fast flowing. Fifteen kilometres into our day, we hit another waterfall that Alfy had marked on the GPS. A few fishermen had shouted to warn us just before we reached it, but we knew it was coming. This was lucky, as it appeared very suddenly around a blind corner, following on from a series of calm rock pools that gave no hint of what was up ahead. For the past few days, locals had been warning us that two South African kayakers had been drowned at this spot the year before. We got as close as we could safely get to the drop, then unloaded and carried the Klepper down the rock face to the side of the waterfall.

Figure 25 – Portage with the Klepper (28 June 2016)

We decided to have lunch at the foot of the waterfall, in the shade of a lone tree that had somehow managed to take root in the grey rocks. The meal involved ploughing through all of the remaining food that did not need cooking: biscuits, lollipops, a cut of biltong, some peanuts and a can of soft drink each. Hardly a balanced diet, but it did not matter: that night we could cook up a storm and the following day we would be walking through populated areas on the other side of Capanda Dam, able to buy all sorts of fresh produce. As we ate, I made a video diary entry:

'This is our absolute final obstacle and it's quite a significant one. So we just need to carry the boat round this and then, just over there I believe, are calm waters.'

With a belly full of food and an agreed plan of attack, it felt good to be celebrating this milestone with Alfy.

It is a shame that I would be proved so wrong.

WOULD YOU LIKE TO BUY SOME DIAMONDS?

Once we had walked down this final elevation change, we entered the Capanda Dam floodplain. Construction of the Soviet-designed dam began in 1987, at the height of the Angolan Civil War. It was occupied by UNITA forces between 1992 and 2000, who seriously damaged parts of the dam in an effort to blow it up. The installation was not brought fully online until after the civil war had ended, in 2004. It remains Angola's largest single source of electricity, with an installed capacity of 520MW. When the reservoir was finally filled, it created a 45km-long floodplain that is 10km wide in places, clearly visible in satellite photography. Whole communities had to be relocated, causing some controversy.

The route from the foot of the waterfall to the dam itself was relatively straightforward. What we had not counted on was the lack of current in this area: the water was completely still. There was also a very strong headwind across the vast, flat expanse of water. Combined, this served to drag our average speed down by at least 2km per hour.

Paddling towards the dam was laborious in the midday heat. To make matters worse, our kayak was followed by a thick cloud of biting insects as we paddled along and no amount of DEET or wind would dissuade them. These aggressive creatures buzzed around our heads, flying up nostrils and into ears, biting any exposed skin they could access. Soon our arms and legs were a patchwork of bumps and bloody dots. Our pace slowed further as the heat and biting sapped our energy.

As the sun set, our spirits were briefly lifted as we saw the *Pedras Negras* on the horizon. Officially known as the Black Rocks at Pungo Andongo, these mysterious columns of granite rock dominate the flat surrounding savannah, rising between 70 and 200m into the air. The rocks are a long day trip from Luanda, 315km to the west. Visitors can not only marvel at the impressive geological formations, but also see the supposed footprints of Queen Nzinga preserved in the rock.

Queen Nzinga came to the throne of the Mbundu people in the Kingdom of Ndongo in 1624. She then expanded her influence by conquering the neighbouring Kingdom of Matamba, to the east, in 1631. Having cut her teeth as a diplomat under her brother Ngola

Mbande's rule, Nzinga is widely celebrated in Angolan history for having bravely resisted the Portuguese colonisation of Angola's interior in the mid-seventeenth century. Over two centuries later, in December 1854, Scottish explorer David Livingstone spent a few weeks here recovering from a bout of severe rheumatic fever, during his trans-continental expedition.

Great views and historical links aside, all of these added delays meant we had no hope of making it to the dam that night. We rounded a large peninsula and decided to camp on a rocky island, 200m off the south bank of the river. On the north bank, at least 750m away, we could see the bright lights of an industrial complex. A pumping station also rose out of the centre of the river nearby. It was odd to see a building of this scale by the side of the Kwanza, but we had to remind ourselves that the isolated section of the river was now behind us. There were populations of people all along it from now until the Atlantic Ocean.

The building we were staring at belonged to Biocom, a Brazilian firm that produces sugar, ethanol fuel and electricity derived from biomass. Behind the building, which must have housed pumps to move water from the river to their plantations, was an 81,201-hectare plantation, part of the Capanda Agro-Industrial Complex.

Our home for the night was the rocky summit of a hill. The rest of the hill, along with the surrounding land, had long since been submerged. It was a small island, ten metres at its widest point, with a flat landing area and then a plateau with a few trees growing on it. Some fishermen had obviously had the same idea as us: up on top we found the remnants of a fire and a hut made of logs.

From our evening perch, much of the landscape around us looked like an optical illusion. We were far higher up than nature had intended us to be. There was even a submerged forest in front of us, with only the tips of the tallest trees poking out a metre or so from the water's surface. With the reassuring hum of the Biocom pumps in the background, we set about preparing the camp.

We were both exhausted from battling against the headwind, but Alfy was looking particularly rough by the time we got ashore. He had caught the sun and the insects had absolutely destroyed his head, arms and torso. He complained of not feeling very well, but still pressed on with unloading the Klepper. I walked to the top of the hill to set up the tents.

'Hey, Oscar, come and look at this.'

Alfy had unloaded all of the gear from the interior of the Klepper and noticed a lot of water in the rear sections, litres in fact. Perhaps this had contributed to our slowing pace that day. After flipping the kayak over and emptying it, we soon saw the cause of the issue: there were numerous holes in the skin from smashing into submerged rocks in the rapids. Armed with a roll of Gorilla tape, some Patex glue purchased in Camacupa and neatly cut sections of tyre inner tube, Alfy patched her up as best he could.

We even had a large tear in the nose section of the Klepper, under the waterline. This must have been opened up the day before in the rapids. Any earlier and we would have noticed. Of all the places to spring a leak, this was not a good one: the widest point on the entire river. We had been over half a kilometre from the bank at times. Alfy noted that we should keep an eye on the problem the following day and possibly adjust our route to stay closer to the banks.

'I really don't feel very well.' Alfy sat down, head in his hands, by the waterline.

'What's wrong, mate?' I was immediately worried. It was very unusual for Alfy to complain and he looked terrible.

'I'm so itchy. I think it's those bugs. Can you take a look?'

With that he lifted up his shirt. Both his chest and back were covered with a distinctive, bright red v-shaped rash. It looked like an allergic reaction. With that he lay down on the rocky ground, as if to sleep. I grew increasingly concerned as I looked over the water to the Biocom compound.

Camping on an island had been a terrible idea. If Alfy was collapsing, how would I get him to help? Loading him into the Klepper then kayaking solo across the water in the dark would be risky. Even if I could get him to the building with lights, there was no guarantee there would be people there to help. It might just be an automated pumping station. The satellite photography had shown the complex stretching back 15km from the waterline, and who knew where the workers were within that area. Could I load him on the buggy and drag him perhaps?

My first approach was to try and fix things on the island. I had Alfy drink some rehydration mixture and take some anti-allergens. For the worst-case scenario, Alfy going into anaphylactic shock, I loaded up an Epinephrine (adrenaline) syringe and hunted around for our intravenous drip, which we had considered offloading at the INAD army base by Kuito Bridge. While collecting firewood to keep the insects away, I hoped and prayed it would not come to using the serious medical gear.

After half an hour of being very still, Alfy began to perk up. He was talking again and had regained his appetite. The bright rash on his back had also subsided, although it was still visible. Sun exposure, dehydration and insect bites had likely combined to bring this on, but it seemed to be a manageable condition.

To celebrate Alfy's return to health, we cooked up the chorizo that I had bought in the shops by Malanje Bridge. This was another mistake: eating unrefrigerated meat-based produce in a tropical climate with no sell-by date printed on the packaging. The meal stayed in my system for about ten minutes before being violently ejected. We both went to bed feeling fragile that night.

Wednesday, 29 June was definitely the day we would hit Capanda Dam. Alfy and I both felt much better after the issues the previous night. The gentle hum of the pumping station had remained with us all night, and in the morning the lights on the other side of the river cut through the fog. Dead, preserved branches of the drowned forest stretched up out of the water in front of us. This was a new obstacle we had to be wary of: a sharp branch could puncture the Klepper's skin. The five patches Alfy had stuck on the holes had dried overnight. Now they needed to stay waterproof for the remaining 40km of paddling before the dam and the 220km after it.

Our second day of approaching the dam was just as hard as the first. The wind billowed in our faces and we had to dig deep to make forward progress. It even blew up waves on this section that had us rocking up and down in the battered Klepper, slapping the nose against the surface as we crashed down another face. All I could think about was the tear in the front and whether it would hold. After five hours of paddling we paused for lunch in a less windy stretch. But we had run out of food that we could eat without cooking. Our lunch that day was a lollipop each, scavenged from a random bag in the cabin. We needed to get to the dam quickly.

Figure 26 – Running out of food (29 June 2016)

It took us all day to cover the 40km to Capanda, which was unusually slow progress.

'How do you fancy our chances of getting people to watch a documentary of this journey?' I asked Alfy, pointing around us. 'I mean, it's all a bit samey here, isn't it?'

'Yeah, it's going to be a tough sell. Maybe we could make it a radio show? You know I tried that a few years ago with BBC Radio 4's *Journey of a Lifetime*. Got through to the last five, but then didn't get selected.'

'What was your suggested journey?'

'I applied to head to Nauru in the Pacific, where my dad used to be British Honorary Consul. I wanted to look at the impacts of phosphate strip mining there in the 1960s and 1970s. You know they used to have the highest GDP per capita in the world thanks to all the mineral resources and now they've trashed the island?'

It sounded like an incredible journey. I could not help but see the parallels to the diamond mining happening all around us. Great wealth for the few, at great cost to the many.

In the end, we did not paddle up to the dam, partly because of safety concerns but also because we doubted the Angolan authorities would appreciate two foreigners getting near their prized hydroelectric installation. About 4km before the dam we veered off to the north, aiming for a waterfront village that Alfy had visited before, which gave access to the main road west. Even paddling past from this distance, the dam was an awe-inspiring sight: a wing shape, stretching 1.3km across the river and forcing it all through a 100m opening to drive the turbines.

We arrived in the village just before dark. It was a simple assortment of wooden and mud-brick huts, with a patch of reeds that they moored their boats in. Some fishermen had just returned home with the catch of the day and welcomed us enthusiastically. We purchased four fish from them, as they gutted their catch by the waterside. I jokingly asked if these were the type of fish that tasted of mud.

'Oh no!' they reassured me, laughing. 'These are very good fish!'

Our first move was to ask to see the *soba*, who they said was up in Capanda town at the time. The men of the village all gathered round and engaged in an animated discussion about whether we could camp there. For a minute, there was a risk that *confusão* would break out, but luckily an older man named Helder intervened to save the situation.

The conclusion was that we could camp there, but we needed to speak to the *soba* on the phone to confirm arrangements and ensure our presence was registered with the authorities. This all seemed like a sensible precaution given our proximity to a hydroelectric installation. The Angolan government tends to be a little sensitive about 'strategic sites' such as bridges, power stations, oil facilities and dams since the civil war. After all, UNITA had even tried to blow this dam up during the fighting.

Unfortunately, we had no phone signal down by the water and even after heading up the hill, none could be found. Helder, clearly one of the more senior men in the village, told us not to worry. He would hike into Capanda and tell the *soba* and the authorities about our presence. We could go and meet them in the morning to explain what we were doing and show our documentation and permits. Everyone was happy with this compromise and the group soon dispersed, giving us a chance to buy some fresh fish and set up our tents.

Soon we were tucking into some delicious foil-wrapped fish with rice and rehydrated beans, plotting our hiking route on the GPS for the following day. The fishermen had been right: these were good fish! We sat on a log in the middle of the village and a few of the inhabitants joined us for dinner. We chatted about our route so far and what lay ahead. None of the fishermen had ever seen a hippo west of the Capanda Dam. We went to bed thinking the hard work was already behind us; but it was only just beginning.

Arrested at Capanda

Our arrest was as sudden as it was shocking. Shouting. Rifle barrels in our tents. Dragged out and handcuffed. Alfy getting a knee in the back of the head. Our tents and possessions ripped up and thrown in the back of the police 4×4. Only Alfy's mobile phone managing to evade confiscation.

In the space of five minutes we had gone from fast asleep in our tents to being handcuffed at gunpoint by torchlight. The drive into Capanda was freezing cold. The police had wedged us into the back of the pickup, and with our hands cuffed it was difficult to hold onto anything for support as we bounced up the dirt road. Our tents had been hastily rolled up with all our gear inside and thrown in a separate vehicle. We had no idea if we would be seeing them again. The police chief and his most senior assistant had taken the cab of our 4×4, leaving us crammed into the back with five other officers, three in uniform and two in plain clothes. One kept resting the barrel of his Uzi on the floor. It clanked loudly every time we hit a pot hole. Hopefully he had the safety catch on. The rest of them had AK-47s, pointed more safely up at the night sky.

One of the plain-clothes security officials started trying to bond with us. We thought it best to humour him, not knowing how senior he was or his relationship to the commander.

'Where are you from? You guys have children back home?' He was speaking in broken English.

We told him a bit about our backgrounds, and he was very surprised to hear that neither of us was married or had children. In our early thirties and unmarried? We were well behind schedule by rural Angolan standards. He pointed to one of the uniformed police and sneered. 'This one? Eleven children. He just can't stop fucking!'

Even without speaking the language, the rest of the passengers understood the accompanying crude hand gestures and burst into laughter. We smiled awkwardly. Who were these people and what exactly did they want?

Alfy and I remained calm at this stage. While it was the first time either of us had been handcuffed in Angola, it was not our first experience of detention by armed officials. They likely just wanted to emphasise their authority, assuage the egos of the men in charge. We would probably get our documents checked then be released. Perhaps it was a ploy to extract cash from us. Either way, we could not see it causing too much of a delay.

We wound our way up the dirt road, back towards the dam, before we hit street-lit asphalt. They drove us into a secure gated compound, past row upon row of prefabricated housing, there for the engineers working on the dam. We pulled up at a police station, itself enclosed in another layer of wall. Harsh stadium lighting illuminated the entire compound.

The police chief stepped out of the cab, ushered us inside and presented us to a more senior commander, also in police uniform. We immediately asked why we had been detained.

'Where are your documents?' he barked. The man was tall, overweight and looked like he had just woken up, although his uniform was in good condition.

Still handcuffed, we fished them out of our bags which had now been brought into the police station and laid in a pile on the floor. Alfy leafed through all the permits, pointing them towards the relevant section of the permit from the Ministry of Water and Energy that specifically stated we would be camping in the location we were picked up in. A few other police officers wandered in from adjacent buildings, keen to find out what all the commotion was about this late at night.

'We will copy and verify all of these tomorrow. Until then, you will be held here.'

A night in the police cells did not sound appealing. We protested as best we could: we had all the necessary permits, we both had valid visas, we were trying to help clear landmines in Angola. All to no avail. They refused to give us back the satellite phone so that we could inform the British or Italian embassies about our detention, or the HALO Trust for that matter. The whole experience was frustrating, but we were so exhausted by this stage that we gave up the fight quickly.

Eventually, the commander ordered his men to take the cuffs off our wrists but refused to budge on the detention. He said they had no space in the cells (which was ominous) so we would be kept in the next door medical centre. We were escorted over there by four policemen. It was a prefabricated building with a reception area, a bathroom, an office space and a store cupboard for medical equipment. The place was a little dusty but looked unused. The policemen dragged in a few mattresses and settled in for the night on the floor of the reception area, weapons laid in a pile in the centre of the room.

Figure 27 – Live updates from police custody (29 June 2016)

'Where do you expect us to sleep?'

They gestured to the store cupboard, which at least afforded some privacy and a few less mosquitoes. Alfy and I shuffled in and unfurled our camping mats. The room was three metres deep by six metres wide, with shelving along two sides. Each section had a label indicating what was intended to be stored there: drips, painkillers, antimalarials, diarrhoea treatment, bandages etc. The shelves were bare, save for a huge box of condoms and some HIV awareness posters. It was sad to see the healthcare sector in this state, in one of the richest countries in Africa.

Hands now free, Alfy reached into his side pocket and fished out his mobile phone. In the rush to drag him out of his tent they had neglected to search him. He quickly set about informing everyone he could about our current situation. We even had 3G signal due to our proximity to Capanda! Better yet, I had managed to bring my GoPro camera into the cupboard, rolled into my sleeping bag. That night we recorded a bizarre diary-cam update before trying to get a few hours of sleep. Perhaps calmer heads would prevail in the morning.

At this stage we had little idea of the ordeal that had started in the middle of that night. We went to sleep imagining at worst a day of delay – which would have been enough of a problem to our journey. What actually lay ahead of us defied credulity. Four days of being bounced from authority to authority, accused, interrogated, pleading unsuccessfully with each of them to see the situation with a bit more logic and compassion. We would end up all the way back in Luanda, imprisoned and on the brink of deportation... now that, we had never even imagined.

Purgatory at the police station

We were woken up on Thursday, 30 June by the sound of police officers parading on the concrete square outside in their heavy boots. I walked out into the reception area, stepped over the pile of rifles in the middle of the room and straight out the door. All of our guards were still fast asleep. Alfy made a bit of noise closing the cupboard door and one by one they stirred, grabbed their rifles and headed out to get their commander. He soon came striding back in, angry as usual.

'I have been speaking to my *chefe* about you. Show us your documentation again.'

As before, we laid out all of our paperwork in a pile on the floor, talking him through each piece in meticulous detail. We slowly began to realise that it did not matter how much evidence we showed this man, he was very unlikely to cooperate with us. He photographed each piece of paper with his mobile, then sent it to someone via WhatsApp.

'Now that we have shown you we have permission to be here, please can you let us go? We have a lot of hiking to do today and we do not want to get behind schedule.' I already knew the answer before I asked the question.

'You two did not have permission to be there! You were camping at a strategic site. The dam is off limits to foreigners!' The commander was genuinely angry at our failure to agree with his assessment of the situation. He seemed to see our presentation of documentary evidence and requests for release as an attempt to question his authority.

Alfy offered to show him our tracking data. 'We were never anywhere near the dam. We deliberately stayed many kilometres away from it, I can show you on my screen if you allow us to get the GPS device out. Also, we have specific written permission to be in that location. Why would the ministry give us permission to do something illegal?'

The commander was not interested in GPS evidence. He also had an odd obsession with ensuring that we could see our bags at all times, but not allowing us to touch them or access our gear. He had instructed his men the night before not to allow us to open the bags, even though they were in the reception area with everyone. It had only been out of the personal kindness of one of the guards that we were able to access our anti-malarial medication.

The commander continued this policy today, so the GPS device was off-limits. Perhaps he was worried about accusations of impropriety against his men with regard to our personal belongings. We certainly had a lot of equipment that would prove useful to someone working out in this remote environment. Temporarily content with his WhatsApp photos, the commander walked out of the door, eyes glued to his screen.

An older police officer walked in with a tray containing lemongrass tea, sugar, fresh bread rolls and local honey. He smiled at us.

'We heard you stayed with us last night. You must be hungry.'

Our eyes lit up at this act of kindness. This was the first time we had seen fresh bread on the entire trip and it looked delicious. Also, our bodies were still crying out for sugars, so the honey was a welcome treat. We thanked him profusely and wolfed down the offering.

'Oh, wow! I can get you some more from the canteen if you want?'

We nodded enthusiastically, mouths still full. When the officer returned with another tray, he introduced himself as Flávio. We spent the next hour sat there with him, talking. He asked about the journey we had made thus far and how long we thought the final section would take. Interestingly, Flávio also wanted to know about our lives back in Europe.

'What is this Brexit you are doing? I heard this term on the BBC World Service this morning. I used to listen to this in Portuguese but now that has ended. We must listen in English to try and practise our English skills.'

It was a true test of our language ability to try and explain the workings of the organisation the UK was trying to leave and which bits they still wanted access to!

In turn, we asked Flávio what life was like protecting the communities around the dam and how large an impact the drop in oil price had had on this part of Angola. As the bare shelves in the medical unit implied, life had not been easy for this community since late 2014.

'The economy causes many problems for us today. We do not have the equipment we need. The doctor has not visited this medical centre for many months and you see that there is no medical equipment. Also, they do not pay our salaries on time. *Muita confusão.*'

Even the police were struggling to get the equipment they needed to do their jobs (especially paying for fuel). Someone shouted Flávio's name outside, so he wished us good luck with our current predicament, made his apologies and left.

The commander came marching back in with two policemen, pointed to our pile of gear and told them to load it all onto one of the Land Cruisers.

'I have just spoken to my *chefe*. He wants to meet you in person to discuss this issue.'

This suggestion worried us both. As far as we were concerned there was nothing to discuss. We had cooperated fully, provided all our permits and visas for authentication and now needed to be getting on our way.

'Please can we speak to your boss on the phone? We have a long way to hike today and cannot afford to get behind schedule by driving to see him.'

'My boss does not discuss issues like these on the phone. He insists that you be brought to him in Malanje. Get in the vehicle.'

Up the ladder of Angolan authority

Malanje, the provincial capital, was 135km to the east, back the way we had just paddled from! This would be a major delay. Any residual optimism we had from the night before had vanished. We were now being illegally detained and our passports were confiscated. They piled us into the back of the 4×4, Alfy in the cab and me in the back with three policemen, and away we sped towards Malanje.

The drive was very cold with the early morning air billowing over us. The driving was hair-raising. Whoever was behind the wheel seemed to think that putting on the police siren meant abjuration of any responsibility to stay on the correct side of the road. The only good thing about barrelling along at 130kmph was that the journey was over quickly. Soon, we were racing back past the *Pedras Negras* we had seen the day before. A barefoot boy stood by the side of the road holding up a large rat tied to a stick. They both looked at us with forlorn stares.

'Those rats are excellent in stew,' one of the police officers commented, 'I shall get one on the way home. This province has really excellent rats.'

Malanje is 375km east of Luanda. Following the breakdown of the elections in 1992, the city found itself completely surrounded by UNITA troops. The population was shelled and faced starvation due to blockade. Today, the central plaza features a haunting memorial to this period: a number of AK-47s, half buried in a black rock garden, pointed up at the skies. The defensive rings of landmines that government troops laid around the provincial capital are still being cleared to this day.

Our vehicle rolled straight into the provincial police headquarters, just behind the beautifully maintained municipal gardens and the provincial governor's office. The police diligently unloaded all our gear, eager for us to take note of the care with which it was being treated. The bags and Klepper were stacked neatly in the courtyard, then they all drove off. We were left to sit in a waiting area by the front gate and try to explain our situation to the policeman guarding the entrance. We were asked to wait and informed that the senior officials in the police station knew that we had arrived and would be with us shortly.

Alfy immediately set to work on his mobile phone. First, he contacted his local partner Osvaldo, who had helped with setting up our permissions for the expedition from the Ministries of the Environment, Tourism plus Water and Energy. Osvaldo's uncle was the Governor of Malanje Province, so he had a lot of high-level access to security officials. He messaged Alfy back immediately and confirmed that he was working hard to sort out the issue from his end.

Alfy also messaged his girlfriend Marie-Louise and his driver Garcia, asking if they were free to come over to Malanje and bring some food supplies. Although the circumstances had changed, Marie-Louise had always planned to drive out and meet us at some point on the final stretch of river, for one last resupply. She jumped at the chance to see Alfy again and set out from Luanda that morning.

Meanwhile, there was little we could do but sit outside that police station and wait.

Osvaldo called later that morning.

'You guys are in a lot of trouble. Someone has opened a criminal investigation into you, which is registered here on the police systems in Luanda. Immigration are also involved now. You need to speak to the National Police Commander in the Province, Comissário António José Bernardo.'

At around lunchtime, the cavalry arrived in the form of Marie-Louise and Garcia.

Garcia, looking smart as usual, was very concerned about the whole situation. He paced up and down in the waiting area in his striped blue-and-white shirt, commenting on the madness of the whole situation.

'This cannot be right. If they have the correct documentation, then surely it is not correct to detain them like this?'

The policeman on reception shook his head, disinterested. Garcia was asking the wrong person.

Marie-Louise took a more British stiff-upper-lip attitude to the whole affair.

'They have made a mistake and it will take a while to correct. We just have to be patient.' In the meantime, we tucked into her delicious home-made sandwiches.

Immigration and the real Chefe

A few hours later, we were told that *Serviço de Migração e Estrangeiros* (SME), the immigration authorities, wanted to speak to us.

There was no need for more handcuffing. They still had our passports and all our expedition equipment, so we were going nowhere without them. Garcia drove us over to a dusty pink colonial building in front of a petrol station on the road out of town.

A battered wooden door led into a narrow hallway that then opened up into a courtyard, with offices off four sides. There was a little shade over on one side by their noticeboards. In it, a Chinese husband and wife were sat on the floor, looking stressed. Our possessions were brought in, placed in a pile in the corner and photographed. We sat down on the floor next to the Chinese couple and waited to see what would happen next.

We spent the next six hours in this courtyard, or being interrogated by Marcos and Felizardo, a pair of security officials who introduced themselves as 'from the immigration authorities'.

It turned out they were from the *Serviço de Investigação Criminal* (SIC), the investigative appendage to Angola's police force.

Marcos and Felizardo took their jobs seriously, but were more jovial than the police. Marcos was a very small man, in an oversized green suit. Felizardo was a typical portly security official, complete with a bright white polo shirt that barely managed to conceal his gut. With the help of a typist we were never introduced to, they called us into an interrogation room individually and asked us to recount all the events that had brought us to Capanda Dam, right from the beginning.

At no stage was their questioning accusatory. In fact, at times they would laugh or exclaim in disbelief as I recounted some of the more outlandish aspects of our adventure. At the end of it all, they handed over the typed-up statement and told us to sign it. There was no suggestion that we were entitled to consult with a lawyer.

While all this was going on, Osvaldo was working hard in Luanda trying to secure us a meeting with the Governor of Malanje. As the most senior political figure in the province, he might be able to secure our release. By this stage, we had also contacted the British Embassy and informed them of our detention.

Figure 28 – Our gear is photographed by SIC officials in Malanje SME building (30 June 2016)

David Pert, the Head of Public and Corporate Services at the British Embassy, was the contact Alfy had on his phone. At the time, we believe he was the most senior British diplomat in the country. David and Alfy knew each other quite well and people at the British Embassy (including the Deputy Ambassador and his wife) had been tracking our daily progress via the website.

In between our discussions with the officials, we met with the Head of SME in Malanje, Mr Silvestre Apolinário Cassinda.

From our very first encounter, it was clear that we were not going to get along. He treated us with the same arrogance and disdain as he treated all of his staff.

We had seen him outside the building, texting on his phone earlier that day, and had approached him to ask if he could help us.

'I am not at work right now. Do not speak to me.' With that, he had walked back inside.

He was never without his leather attaché case and at least two mobile phones. Apolinário was bald, in a dark-green safari suit with long pointy brown shoes and matching accessories. The watch on his wrist looked expensive. His eyes appeared half closed and he had a disconcerting habit of looking past you, or at his phone.

'Is there a problem with our immigration status or visas?'

'No. But you are under investigation and must remain here.'

'Who is investigating us?'

'The Angolan authorities.'

'But who exactly? What are the charges against us?'

'This is not information we can release to you at this time.'

With that he walked off, ignoring any follow-up questions.

It was becoming increasingly apparent that we would be detained for the night. Apolinário was keen to hand us back over to police custody.

We were allowed to book a hotel in town. Our possessions however, would remain in SME custody for 'security purposes' until the matter was resolved.

Despite the access to a shower and clean sheets in the hotel (both very welcome at this stage), we continued to sport the filthy clothes we had been wearing since our arrest in Capanda.

We headed back over to the main police station to tell them which hotel we would be staying in. Apolinário accompanied us over, despite our insistence that his presence was not necessary. Comissário António José Bernardo finally appeared.

José Bernardo looked like a grizzled security forces veteran. He had creased cheeks, broad shoulders and a confident stance. Unlike many of the other security officials we had been dealing with, he looked as though he was physically capable of chasing down a suspect and detaining them. He was wearing a leather jacket with the insignia of the Malanje Police on his epaulettes and a smartly pressed blue uniform underneath. His beret was well fitted and he sported a pair of thin-framed glasses.

The police chief shook hands firmly with us both and got straight to the point.

'I know who both of you are. We have had meetings about you today. Let me say this from the start: your expedition will be ending here today in Malanje.'

Definitely not the start we had been hoping for. Apolinário nodded his head in approval.

José Bernardo glanced casually at our documents as we handed them over, but he had already made up his mind.

'Nobody told me about this expedition. This is unacceptable! I must be consulted about any activities such as yours that enter my province of responsibility. Where are your permits from my department here in Malanje?'

At the provincial boundary at Malanje Bridge near Cangandala, the night we camped at the police checkpoint, we had shown them all our documentation and Comandante Paulo had radioed in our position. We could even show them photographic and video evidence of our presence at the checkpoint.

José Bernardo was not impressed. 'No, this is not enough.'

He then leafed through our documentation again, looking for some other flaw to pick up on. 'Also, your visas are incorrect. You need expedition visas for a journey such as this.'

There was no such thing as an expedition visa.

'How are you making money from this trip? Who is paying you to do this?'

Throughout the journey, we had struggled to explain our motivations to the Angolan people we met along the way. I suppose it did sound somewhat unbelievable: we were taking a long journey in a slow and inefficient means of transport through a remote area, for no material gain. Quite the opposite in fact: this was costing us thousands of pounds. Neither Apolinário nor José Bernardo believed us.

'They must be here for the diamonds,' Apolinário interjected.

'No, no diamonds! You have all of our gear, you can search for yourselves. You will find no evidence of this accusation. We are here to raise funds for landmine clearance in Angola. That is all. Nobody is paying us.'

The meeting broke up on a sour note. José Bernardo instructed us to stay in Malanje and emphasised that under his authority, our expedition was over.

'Maybe if you go back to Luanda, get the proper permits, maybe then you can come back. But right now, you will not be continuing to kayak anywhere in my province.'

A plea to the Vice-Governor

Just before we went to dinner, there was a glimmer of hope: Osvaldo called Alfy.

'Guys, listen, I have spoken to the Vice-Governor of Malanje Province. He said he is willing to meet you this evening. You must hurry, go to his office immediately!'

We smartened up as best we could. As we climbed into the mirrored lift with Garcia, we became a little self-conscious. Staring back at us were two sunburned, unkempt men in shorts, muddy boots and filthy, stained polo shirts. Plus, our beards were out of control.

Smart attire is very important in Angolan business culture, and it is a sign of disrespect to turn up to a meeting with someone more senior than you and not be smartly dressed.

The secretary looked us up and down in horror, then ushered us into the Vice-Governor's office. He was very tall, dressed impeccably in a pin-stripe black suit and red silk tie. We opened by apologising profusely for our attire, explaining that the immigration authorities had confiscated our gear, including clothing, and refused to give it back. He took it well, apologised for the situation then gestured for us to sit down. We planted ourselves on the black leather sofa, which was cold on our bare skin from the air conditioning set to an icy 16 degrees.

'I am sorry to hear about your situation. The Governor is away from the province right now, but I have been working hard to resolve this issue.'

We explained the ups and downs of our interactions with SME, SIC and the Malanje Police Force. The Vice-Governor listened intently, expressing his condolences for the mess.

'Let me see what we can do to help. You must remember that Angola recently had a war, so we are not prepared for these types of activities in remote areas. Some people still have the wartime mentality. However, I am confident we will get you going again tomorrow.'

This was music to our ears. Whatever Osvaldo had done behind the scenes, it seemed to be working. Just then, the Vice-Governor's phone rang. He excused himself and picked it up.

'Yes, I have them with me here now... No... No, they explained... Oh, I did not realise... yes, OK, I will tell them... OK... Yes, thank you, *camarada*.'

His body language completely changed while he was on the phone. He sat down again. 'This was Comissário José Bernardo. I had not realised that you already met him and that a decision had been made by his department. I apologise, but he says that you cannot continue the journey. This is something for you to discuss with his office tomorrow.'

Just like that, our last sliver of hope vanished. That one phone call had clearly demonstrated who was really in charge.

A plea to the Ministry of Tourism

That night, Alfy, Marie-Louise and I went out for a pizza to take our minds off the situation, but the frustration was palpable. We had made it almost 1,000km, through some of the most remote sections of Angola. We were now on the home straight: some hiking then only 220km of kayaking that Alfy had already done before. The end was in sight and now we were having it snatched away by an officious police commander on an ego trip.

The only positive was that this unscheduled pause in the expedition was giving my feet an excellent opportunity to dry and heal. Regardless, it was still difficult to sleep that night.

On Friday, 1 July we tried our best to remain optimistic. The arbitrary decisions of one official could not end the trip, not after we had come so far. We started the day with an epic buffet breakfast in the hotel restaurant. The other guests must have thought we were very strange: two foreigners in stinking, filthy clothes, stuffing our faces with as many bread rolls as we could lay our hands on.

Whatever was on offer, we were sticking it in a roll and washing it down with generous helpings of coffee. As I was settling into my third serving of fruit salad, a young man came over and introduced himself.

'Hi, my name is Lutete and I work for the Ministry of Tourism.' Already this was promising. He explained that he was down in Malanje shooting some promotional film material for the national parks.

'Have you guys tried the weed down here? Man, it'll blow your mind! I love coming over here from Luanda. The whole province is famous for its weed.'

He had a reassuringly laid-back attitude. We talked about his time studying abroad and his impressions of the Angolan educational system. It was encouraging to hear him talking about a new generation of Angolans heading back to their home country as the economy opened up.

'There are lots of opportunities here that you would not be able to access if you stayed abroad. These people [the Ministry of Tourism] offered me a great gig; there's no way I would have the freedom to make the films I want to make, with these budgets, if I stayed in America or South Africa or even Europe. The only thing is, you got to get used to working on Angolan time and with Angolan officials. These guys can be crazy!'

We explained our situation, and he shook his head knowingly.

'There's that mindset. People just aren't used to having an open society. Permits, permits, permits! Maybe my boss can help you though. He's very senior in the Ministry of Tourism. He'll be down in a minute for breakfast.'

Lutete's producer appeared before his boss, slinking into the restaurant in the same clothes he had worn the night before. There was hushed discussion between the two about his nocturnal exploits, a couple of high-fives, then he headed up to his room to shower just as Lutete's boss came through the door. He was a tiny little man in his late fifties, with thick-rimmed glasses. Alfy and I introduced ourselves.

In a move straight out of Apolinário's playbook, Lutete's boss refused to make eye contact, sat deliberately far away from us, then began lecturing us loudly.

'Oh, I know who you are. We have already had meetings about you two, yesterday. You cannot simply come into our country and expect to behave as you please, to go wherever you wish. There are regulations and procedures in place. The law must be obeyed, or there will be problems, as you are now discovering!'

Lutete looked sheepishly at us with a shrug as we left, clearly used to having to indulge his bosses' rants. No wonder he was keen on all that weed.

We spent the next seven hours in Angolan bureaucratic purgatory. The frustration mounted. With each hour that passed, we were falling further and further behind. The July 11 deadline was fast approaching and we still had a long way to go.

Figure 29 – Trying to keep spirits up outside SME headquarters in Malanje (1 July 2016). Image credit: Marie-Louise Henham

Garcia intervened on our behalf on a few occasions. He was calm, polite and, being an older Angolan man, was able to speak authoritatively to the officials. We were so grateful for everything that Garcia did that day. None of this was part of his job description, but he genuinely felt that what was being done was an injustice and that it reflected poorly on his country.

None of Garcia's impassioned pleas made any difference. By this stage, Comissário José Bernardo had already escalated the issue to the Ministry of the Interior in Luanda and there was nobody within 300km of us who could reverse this decision. The *confusão* had spread and now it was almost irrelevant who had started it. It had taken on a life of its own.

The closer we got to 3pm, the less likely this was to be resolved before Monday. Nothing would get done over the weekend.

We went to visit the officials Marcos and Felizardo to ask why the report was taking so long.

Growing increasingly desperate, we suggested that we continue our expedition and if there were any issues, they always knew where to find us. We were unlikely to escape through hiking and kayaking, especially as they knew our exact route.

'Patience, Oscar, patience. Soon you will be free to go.'

As 3pm came and went, there was still no word from SIC headquarters in Luanda. We had even tried driving over to the Ministry of Water and Energy building to try and get them involved. After all, they had given us the specific permission to camp in the village where we had been arrested. That did no good either.

People were beginning to pack up to go home. We rushed back to SME, to ensure that our expedition gear did not get locked in the building over the weekend. It was still there, next to that sad-looking Chinese couple, who were still being ignored in the corner of the courtyard. We sat down next to it and wondered what to do next.

The British Embassy try to help

Alfy's phone then rang. It was the British Embassy number, so he answered immediately.

'Hello, Alfy? This is Carlos Canjungo, I am the Pro-Consul here at the British Embassy in Luanda. I am going to help with your situation.'

He seemed very confident that the situation could be resolved and did a lot to reassure us that the problems were not insurmountable. Carlos clearly had years of experience dealing with Angolan officialdom and was now our best hope of getting out of Malanje that evening. If we could get back on the road on Saturday morning, then we should be able to finish on schedule.

At around 4pm Apolinário came back in and declared that we needed to get out of his courtyard. When asked where exactly he expected us to go, he made it very clear this was not his problem. He and his staff wanted to go home for the weekend and we could resume our battle on Monday morning. This was completely unacceptable. If we were still stuck in Malanje on Monday, 4 July, there was little hope that we could finish by Monday, 11 July. He was consigning our expedition to failure.

A seated protest

Realising that Apolinário was immune to appeals to reason, or even appeals to due process, we settled on a new tactic: start a sit-in. Alfy pulled up a plastic chair from the corner and sat down in the middle of the courtyard, in the most conspicuous location possible. All the SME staff in every office could now see us.

'We are not moving until you have resolved our situation. We cannot wait until Monday.'

As we expected, Apolinário did not like this at all. Marcos and Felizardo from SIC appeared and tried to persuade us to move.

'Gentlemen, if you will just step outside onto the street, we can discuss this further.'

We knew that if we stepped outside, they would simply lock us out, keeping custody of our gear and passports over the weekend. We calmly explained that we were going nowhere without all our possessions.

More and more junior SME employees were coming out into the courtyard, to see what the fuss was about. From one office, a man in police uniform appeared. As he got closer we recognised him: this was the police commander from Malanje Bridge, Comandante Paulo! Here, in front of us, was a police witness who could testify to the fact that we had registered with the Malanje police authorities upon entering the province. We asked him why he had not informed José Bernardo of this fact, but he quickly walked away without responding. He did not want to get involved in this mess just before the weekend.

Apolinário could barely contain his anger at this stage.

'Look at all of these people who cannot leave because of you! Do you wish to inconvenience them all? You are wasting all of *our* time!'

Apolinário gave us his ultimatum. 'You cannot stay here. If you wish to resolve this issue, you must go back to Luanda. These gentlemen will escort you.'

He gestured to a plain-clothed policeman, semi-automatic sticking conspicuously out of his holster.

Dragged back to Luanda

Luanda was a long way away. At least 375km west. This was not the first time someone had suggested sending us back there (José Bernardo had been very keen on the idea the first time we met him) but this was the first time it was being proposed under threat of force. We got Carlos on the phone again and asked him to speak to Apolinário.

After a few minutes of conversation, the phone was handed back to us and Carlos said solemnly, 'Guys, I'm so sorry, but this has become very serious now. You must do as they say and come back to Luanda.'

The lack of logic in this whole situation was baffling. The plain-clothes police officer was becoming impatient: he understood that Luanda was at least a five-hour drive and driving at night on Angolan roads is dangerous.

'Your bags and your passports will be transported by my representatives here. They will be returned to you once you reach Luanda.'

I asked, 'Are you guaranteeing that this man will return our possessions?'

'Yes, yes, of course,' Apolinário assured us, smiling. 'As soon as you are back in Luanda, you will be released from our custody and your passports and possessions will be returned to you. Just go back to the

SME offices there, register your presence, and then you will then be free to return to your residence in the city, I guarantee you.'

Neither of us believed him.

'I hope you understand what you have done here. We are being treated as criminals, but we have done nothing illegal. We are simply tourists, trying to enjoy this beautiful country and to help with the development of the country through supporting mine clearance. What you have done here is not right.'

There was an awkward silence. Nobody was making eye contact. After a short pause, the workers dispersed back to their offices. Apolinário could finally go home for the weekend.

We jumped into the 4×4 with Marie-Louise and Garcia, absolutely spent from another day of pleading our case. Poor Garcia had a long drive ahead of him. He swapped mobile numbers with the officials who had our passports, and then we headed off in convoy. They were driving a comically small Daihatsu, which somewhat detracted from the menacing look of the armed security official holding our passports to ransom. It also meant we had to load up and carry our gear ourselves, as it would not fit in the Korean vehicle. At least this way we could keep an eye on it.

The SME official driving the car, called Rúben, was pretty upbeat about the whole affair. 'Listen, guys, let's just get back to Luanda, then we can give back all of your stuff and go our separate ways. I just want to get back quickly and finish this business.'

We set out from Malanje just as the sun was going down. The first topic of discussion was what would actually happen once we got back to the SME offices in Luanda. First off, given that our projected arrival time was 11pm, the odds of there being anyone still in the SME offices to register our presence were very slim. Even if there were a few night owls waiting for us, why they would simply register our presence then let us go was beyond us. The whole exercise seemed totally pointless. Perhaps this was just a way of guaranteeing that we left Malanje, so that everyone could tell José Bernardo that they had disposed of those troublesome foreigners?

The route back to Luanda is well paved apart from a few short sections of potholes. Friday night is a terrible time to be driving, as people are just getting off work and drinking on their way to wherever they are spending the weekend.

Angola suffered at least 5,591 road traffic deaths in 2013 according to World Health Organization figures, the fourth highest total in Africa, despite having a population of less than 22 million people at the time. Many of these deaths are caused by drink-drivers. The poor state of many Angolan vehicles and the low driving standards add to the dangers. Garcia handled the journey like a professional though, shouting at the other drivers to be careful where they were driving and avoiding numerous animals in the road in the rural sections. '*Malucos* (crazy),' he grumbled, as another *candongueiro* (local minibus taxi) overtook us round a blind corner.

Three hours into the journey, Garcia's phone rang and he was instructed to pull into the next petrol station. We stopped in the half-lit forecourt, taking this opportunity for a bathroom break. I asked our SME man Rúben what the delay was.

'We just need to wait here for some people.'

'Well, thanks for that clarification. Which people? How long will they be?'

As usual, no further information was offered. As we sat around, we started talking to the young plain-clothes policeman. He was just as frustrated as we were with the whole situation.

We pointed to his weapon. 'Are you going to shoot us if we drive away?' Alfy joked.

'Ha ha, no, no! I have no idea why I am here. *Senhor* Apolinário just called me and said I need to escort you to Luanda. But I am based in Malanje! Nobody told me why, and I have no money for overtime or accommodation when we arrive. They said I need to drop you then come straight back tomorrow. Why are SME telling me what to do anyway? I am police. But my boss said go, so we will have to sleep in the car tonight.'

Half an hour later, a truck pulled up with four Lebanese men in it and another SME official. Rúben walked over with a stack of Lebanese passports, each one with an Emirates airline ticket in it. Hands were shaken, packages exchanged and the next thing we knew, he was back, demanding that we get on the road again.

'Who were they?' I asked, expecting no answer.

'Deportees.' He said matter-of-factly. This all seemed very suspicious, but by now we had learned not to ask too many questions.

A few hours later we were back in Luanda. Thanks to our delay, it was almost midnight. We pulled up at the gates of the SME headquarters. It was a brightly illuminated multi-storey building on Rua Amílcar Cabral, named after the Bissau-Guinean and Cape Verdean independence leader who defeated the Portuguese colonial forces in Guinea-Bissau. As predicted, there was nobody there to greet us. Rúben honked his horn a while, then got on his mobile, but to no avail. Everyone had packed up and gone home for the weekend.

'You need to come with us. We will go to the other headquarters.'

We refused outright. Who knew how long they intended to drive around Luanda, looking for an official who had probably gone home seven hours previously.

'We will head back to Alfy's home tonight. Here is the address. We will meet you back here tomorrow at 8am and we can sort this mess out then.'

Reluctantly, Rúben agreed and Garcia turned the car around. The policeman and Rúben headed off into the night, to find a quiet spot to park and sleep in their ridiculously small car.

Back at Alfy's flat

It was strange walking back into Alfy's flat for the first time in a month, especially under these circumstances. We felt like intruders, as though we were breaking in somewhere we were not supposed to be. Marie-Louise brewed up some tea and we settled into the couch.

'What do you think will happen tomorrow?' I asked Alfy.

'I wouldn't be surprised if they arrested us.'

'No, neither would I.'

Deportation

At 7am on Saturday, 2 July Garcia picked us up at Alfy's flat and drove us over to SME. Before arriving, we informed Carlos at the British Embassy where we were going and how to contact us in the event that we were detained again. We walked into an empty car park and could not get into the building because it too was empty. Rúben and the policeman were nowhere to be seen, despite agreeing to meet us at 8am. I do not know why these things continued to surprise us, but they did. What were they playing at?

After an hour of sitting in the car park, getting strange looks from the building security guards, Rúben called Alfy.

'Are you guys at the SME offices? Excellent. You need to come and meet my boss in his office in Viana. He wants to speak to you.'

Viana is an industrial municipality of Luanda, about 30km southeast from the centre where we were. I had no idea that SME even had a location over there, as it was mainly industrial parks and warehouses.

'But you told us to meet here. You promised we would get our passports back an hour ago!'

'Yes, yes, don't worry. Everything will be fine. Just come to the offices in Viana. We will send you the address.'

Something about what Rúben was saying did not add up. He was being far too friendly considering most SME officers' attitudes to us up until this point. Alfy and I agreed that no good would come from driving out to Viana and told Rúben we were refusing his request. He made a few more attempts to persuade us, then finished by snapping, 'Fine. Then we are coming to get you!'

It turned out Alfy was correct. We were getting arrested. Apolinário had lied to us back in Malanje, and now Rúben was lying to us here in Luanda. We quickly called Carlos and explained our situation.

'Stay there. I will inform the other staff at the embassy and drive over there right now. Do not leave without me!'

It was now a race against time. Who would arrive first? Carlos and the British Embassy or Rúben and his SME goons. Five minutes later we had our answer: Rúben rounded the corner in his ridiculous Hyundai, and behind him he had a blue Land Cruiser filled with six regular police officers, all heavily armed.

'Let me stall them,' Alfy said, as he vanished off to the back of the building. There was a toilet in the lobby that security had let us use earlier on that morning. He got buzzed in again, then locked himself in one of the cubicles.

Rúben stepped out of his car and scanned the car park, looking for Alfy.

'Where is the other one? You were both supposed to be here!' The politeness of the night before had vanished. Rúben was now very angry with us.

'He is just in the toilet, sorry. He has a bad stomach – you know how it is. He will be back in five minutes.'

I wondered how Rúben would react when Alfy did not return in five minutes. I also kept checking the spare phone in my pocket, hoping for an update from Carlos.

'Fine. You get in the back of the vehicle while we wait for him.'

'I would feel much more comfortable waiting for Alfy here on the pavement. Please, he will only be a minute.'

I sat down on the floor, hoping they did not handcuff me.

Five minutes passed and still there was no sign of Carlos, or Alfy. Alfy messaged me on WhatsApp, asking what the situation was. I told him to hold tight a while longer. Rúben was becoming increasingly anxious.

'Where is your friend? We need to leave! My boss demanded that we collect you immediately!'

Still no sign of Carlos.

After another ten minutes, Rúben lost his temper.

'I am sick and tired of you two. I was polite to you in Malanje, but because of your arrogance and uncooperative attitude, we were unable to leave for Luanda until after 5pm and we did not arrive until almost midnight! Now, again, you are refusing to obey a reasonable request.' He turned to the police. 'Can't you just handcuff him and throw him in the vehicle?'

To their credit, the police were actually reluctant to force me into the vehicle. After all, I was speaking calmly and was still sat on the floor posing no threat to anyone.

One of the younger officers, an Uzi strapped around his shoulder, tried to reason with me. 'Sir, please would you get in the vehicle? We will not leave without your friend. But you are making this man very angry by not complying.'

'I promise that I will comply with all of your requests, as soon as my friend comes back. We do not want to cause any problems for you, we just want to leave together.'

Rúben began shouting at the police to manhandle me into the vehicle, but the police told him to wait a few more minutes. He stormed off to his car and made an angry phone call. Meanwhile, I got Carlos on the phone and told him the situation. He asked to be put on the phone with the head of the police group, which I duly did. After a few short words, the phone was handed back to me.

'Oscar, you are being taken to the illegal immigrant detention and deportation centre out in Viana. You must comply with the officers now. Don't worry, we are five minutes away and will be right behind you.'

I texted Alfy, who promptly reappeared from his extended bathroom break. He chirpily sauntered out into the car park, smiling to Rúben as he walked, which made him even angrier.

'You should cuff them both,' Rúben growled as he got into his vehicle to lead the way.

Thankfully the police did not listen to him. We got into the back of the pickup with four police officers. Just as we were about to head out of the SME gate, we saw Carlos appear in a British embassy vehicle, complete with diplomatic plates. They tagged onto our convoy, following conspicuously behind.

In convoy to the detention centre

Driving through the streets of Luanda in a police convoy was a novel experience and not one I would want to repeat. The traffic in the city is terrible, and the driver did his best to combat it through a combination of blaring sirens, aggressive driving and even having the men in the back point their weapons at obstructing traffic. Forty-five minutes later, we pulled into the detention centre, in a dusty field surrounded by Chinese industrial parks.

The detention centre is run by SME. It is the main processing centre in the country, a sprawling compound with armed guards at every entrance. There are seven or eight buildings within the camp, some of them prefabricated office space, others bunkhouses for the staff, and one a holding area with cells and a covered outdoor lobby where suspects are seated before processing. The windows on every side were barred, although it still had an open, airy feel.

We were led into the processing area and told to take a seat. Around us were several frustrated-looking Congolese women, some Chinese construction workers and a few men of Middle Eastern origin. Oddly, they allowed both Carlos and the other British Embassy member of staff to accompany us into the holding area, where most of the detainees were watching a football game on a small flat screen TV on the wall. The driver, a Gurkha guard who appeared to be armed, stayed outside near the car, keeping a close eye on things inside. The man accompanying Carlos introduced himself as David Pert, a senior British national on the Embassy staff.

'I'm so sorry we could not meet under more favourable conditions.'

David had cropped grey hair and was dressed in a smart suit, every bit the British diplomat. Under his arm, as well as a file full of papers, he was carrying a copy of the *Bradt Guide to Angola* that I had helped to write in 2013.

'I thought maybe you could sign it for me, once all this is sorted out!'

I admired his optimism. Alfy and I both shook hands with David, then introduced ourselves to Carlos. It was great to put a face to a name after having talked to him for so long throughout our detention. He was dressed a little more casually, in a polo shirt and jeans, clutching at least two mobile phones. Alfy apologised for dragging him into work on a Saturday.

'Not at all! We will have this situation sorted out quickly, do not worry.'

One at a time, Alfy and I were sent to the desk at the front of the processing area, where two women in police uniform, both barely out of their teens, took our personal details. They were not happy about being at work on the weekend and made their displeasure known through the snail's pace of their work. It took about 40 minutes for them to take our details and fingerprint us.

One of them asked me if I had ever committed a crime in Angola before. I tried to make a joke and said, 'Only the crime of being a tourist.'

She looked up at me sullenly, loudly chewing her gum. 'You need to take this seriously.'

While we were undergoing our soporific interrogation and getting ink all over our fingers, Carlos and David had managed to find someone senior within SME to speak to. We eavesdropped on their conversation in the corner of the room. David began with the question we had been asking for the past few days. 'As a representative of the British government, I would like to know under what grounds these two men are being detained.'

The SME gentleman responded in a defensive and officious tone. 'I do not have the authority to give you this information. The charges against these men are classified. If you have questions about this, then you must follow the official channels and lodge a request for information with the Ministry of the Interior on Monday.'

'So you do intend to detain these men here until Monday?'

'Yes. Those are the instructions I have.'

The SME official made these comments at around 11am that morning. His suggestion, detaining us for 48 hours over the weekend, would have dealt a death blow to our efforts to finish the expedition by 11 July. Worse still, there was no suggestion that we would be released on Monday 4 July, just that the Ministry of the Interior would review our case. Looking around the waiting area, I commented to Alfy, 'These people are not here to have their cases reviewed. They are here to be deported.'

While deportation was a profoundly disappointing outcome from my point of view, for Alfy it could very well have meant damage to his professional reputation. The whole reason we needed to be back in Luanda on 11 July was so that he could spend the next fortnight training up his replacement, doing a country hand-over. A transition without Alfy in the country would have been chaotic for his employer and disastrous for his career.

For the next six hours we were at the mercy of the Orwellian immigration services. The questioning became less and less frequent, the periods waiting in the processing area longer and longer. One official accused us of spying on Capanda Dam. Another brought up issues with our visas. A third talked about police registrations in Malanje and kayaking through sensitive diamond areas. They were clearly getting this from whatever had been written about us back in Malanje. Nobody was interested in listening to our side of the story, nor in viewing the GPS evidence that contradicted their claims.

Carlos's body language changed after every discussion with SME officials. His confidence at the beginning of the morning was slowly eroded by the lack of answers, by the refusal of any official to take responsibility, by the barrage of illogical assertions and easily disprovable lies. Carlos's years of experience working at the embassy, as well as for the United Nations in Angola, was being severely tested. We sat on the chairs talking to David, trying to think of another avenue of attack, but nothing came to mind. David had even tried showing them the Bradt travel guide, commenting on how bad for tourism this treatment was. Nothing was having an effect.

Looking around at the other unfortunates in the waiting area, we reflected on how much worse their situation was than ours. There was no Congolese diplomatic representation fighting these people's corner. They were completely at the mercy of the SME officials, powerless to resist the decisions imposed on them, no matter how arbitrary. Years of xenophobic propaganda in the state-run media had made these immigrants an easy target for the security forces. Nobody was coming to their aid here.

The British government, the Italian government and a few calls to the powers-that-be

Eventually, out of sheer desperation, I suggested to David that we get the Italian government involved. Being a dual national I was just as entitled to Italian diplomatic representation as British.

'That's a great idea,' said David. 'Gianluca is really proactive. I'm sure he can help.' Dr Gianluca Battaglia was the First Secretary of the Italian Embassy in Luanda. In my entire five years of living in Angola, my only interaction with the Italian embassy had been watching one of their diplomats hit on my girlfriend at a party. Still, it could not hurt to try. We looked up the number on Alfy's phone, which was inexplicably still in his custody, and we gave him a call.

Dr Battaglia answered immediately. He was cool, calm and collected, asking first for my Italian passport number and then laying out exactly what he was going to do.

'We need to get the Minister of the Interior involved. Quickly. Do you want me to come down there now?'

Alfy and I both agreed that Dr Battaglia should focus on finding the Minister of the Interior, but that coming to the detention centre was unnecessary. We told him that we had thus far failed to get hold of the minister through Osvaldo's network of contacts.

'Don't worry about that. We play tennis together. I'll call him now.'

I was sceptical as to whether Dr Battaglia would be able to get hold of one of the most important politicians in Angola over a weekend. We could only hope.

As we sat waiting, David suggested another untested avenue. 'I suppose we could also try contacting the office of Isabel Dos Santos, see if we can get some traction there? We processed a UK student visa for one of the secretaries over in her office recently.'

Isabel Dos Santos is one of the daughters of former President Dos Santos. Hailed by Forbes in 2013 as 'Africa's first female billionaire', she is a polarising figure in Angola thanks to her extensive network of businesses that encompass banking, retail and telecommunications. Some say she is a shining example of female African entrepreneurship. Others point to her as a shining example of nepotism, alleging that she profits from contracts awarded by the state through her political connections. Financial controversy aside, if anyone could get hold of the Minister of Interior, it would be her. David stepped outside to make some calls.

And then we waited. More hours spent on the seats, looking at the disgruntled Congolese women and the Lebanese businessmen busted working on a tourist visa. Carlos came back from yet another meeting with one of the SME reps. The news was not good.

'Guys, I'm really sorry, but it looks as though you are going to have to spend the night here, maybe even the whole weekend.'

When Carlos gave up hope, we knew things were bad. We were so tired by this stage that we were not even worried any more. The thought of being locked up with dozens of other deportees was far less of a concern than the idea that our expedition was over. We had failed. Almost 1,000km of paddling and hundreds of kilometres of hiking, only to fail at the beginning of the 'easy' third section of the expedition. We hoped Comissário Bernardo one day realised what his ego was costing us and Angolan mine-clearance efforts.

Alfy ran his hands through his hair, then sank his head into his hands, staring at the floor. 'I just can't believe that they are doing this to us.'

We were both sent back to the teenage police officers at the front of the hall to get our final details taken before they took us into the cells. David and Carlos apologised. We had not heard from Dr Battaglia. It was all over.

The large, officious SME commander who had dismissed David's questions earlier came into the room. He explained to David and Carlos that he was taking us into custody and that they could visit again the following day if they wanted to. It was late afternoon now and they needed to leave. Then his phone rang.

Alfy picked up on the change in body language before I did. The commander sprang to attention.

'*Si, chefe… Si… Claro… Si chefe… Imediatamente!*'

Whoever was at the other end of the line was both angry and very important. The commander put his mobile away and immediately jumped into panicked action. He ran up to the police officers interrogating us. 'You don't need to do any more of this. Stop!'

He grabbed the sheets they had been writing our details on. Next, he clicked his fingers and some underlings appeared.

'Fetch their gear. I want it outside by this diplomat's car, now.'

Then he addressed us directly. Gone was the sneer and the arrogance.

'Please follow me, and we will fetch your passports from my office. You are free to leave now.'

Our departure from that facility was a complete blur. We went from being detained for the weekend to being thrust out of the front entrance in a matter of minutes. Nobody ever explained why we had been detained, what charges we were facing or what Angolan laws we had broken on our expedition. We also never found out exactly why we were released (despite making numerous enquiries). Had it been Dr Battaglia's contacts or David's? Perhaps both? It did not matter. Either way, the Ministry of the Interior had intervened and we were released.

Freedom

It was a surreal moment in our expedition. The relief was palpable for both of us, but at the same time, things happened so quickly that we had little time to process. I felt numb, very cautious of raising our hopes again. Our first concern remained: can we still finish?

We jumped into the Land Cruiser with the Gurkha driver. David offered to drop us off at Alfy's apartment. On the way back, we stopped at a petrol station and bought a warm can of Gordon's pre-mixed gin and tonic each to celebrate.

As we toasted in the back of the car, David offered us some advice. 'I don't know what all that was, lads, but if I were you I'd keep your heads down until Oscar leaves the country in a few days. Oh, and for God's sake, don't go back out on the river!'

Alfy smiled but said nothing. Our expedition was not finished yet.

Figure 30 – Alfy celebrates our release (2 July 2016)

A covert expedition

On Sunday, 3 July we woke up at the crack of dawn in Alfy's flat, overlooking the Chicala waterfront in Luanda. From Alfy's balcony we could see the sixteenth-century Fortress of São Miguel high on the hilltop overlooking the sea. Directly in front of his building, the entire *musseque* (slum) had recently been demolished to make room for a new waterfront development. A couple of former residents were busy picking through the remains of their former homes. A security guard, posted on the site to ensure none of the evicted people tried to reoccupy the land, looked on with disinterest.

This was our second chance. After another troubled night reflecting on the madness at the deportation centre, things were coming into clear relief: we simply had to finish the expedition.

Marie-Louise woke up to find us both hunched over satellite photos of the Kwanza River in the living room.

'I do hope you're not doing what I think you're doing...'

We were. There was no question as to whether we would try and complete the expedition if released. The only issue now was: how could we finish before the authorities realised that we were back on the river? The whole situation felt ridiculous: here we were, watching the sunrise while planning a covert operation to kayak the last 220km of the river, when we had done nothing wrong. There should have been no reason to fear the authorities but our experience in Malanje had shown how disruptive even one arbitrary official could be.

Our detention had cost us three days of travel time, which we now needed to make up. Also, who knew how Comissário Bernardo might react to discovering that we had driven straight back onto his patch, in direct defiance of his wishes. Something told me he would not let the small matter of a Ministry of Interior exoneration stop him from detaining us again.

Both Marie-Louise and Garcia thought the plan was crazy, but they were still supportive. Over another generous breakfast with lashings of coffee, Kayak The Kwanza Mark II was born. We would drive back east and re-enter the Kwanza in a secluded location. We would avoid population centres and not tell anyone what we were doing. If fishermen asked what we were up to, we would tell them that we were day-trippers from Luanda, out for a few hours but packing up and heading home that evening. We would set up camp in the dark and set off at daybreak, hiding our fire from outside view. There was one checkpoint on the water with a police boat, which we were going to have to sneak through, but other than that, we hoped to cover the 220km and be in the Atlantic before the authorities realised what had happened, especially as we were re-starting the kayaking on a Sunday.

That Sunday morning it took three hours for Garcia to drive us back to the furthest navigable point on the Kwanza before the dams (where we would have been paddling from had the authorities not detained us). The risk was huge, and the journey mostly silent. Neither of the embassies knew we were doing this. We did not want to put them in the difficult situation of knowing in advance.

I sent a message to my brother and Steph as we drove out, explaining the plan. We would be maintaining radio silence for the remainder of the journey. As far as everyone following the trip around the world was concerned, we were still in Luanda sorting out our paperwork to try and continue. There would be no further Twitter updates and no more movement on our tracker map, as we would stop texting our GPS coordinates to it from now on. Who knew whether the authorities were monitoring our web presence after the arrest?

Late that morning, Garcia pulled us up in a secluded spot by the Kwanza. This was the end of the line for the 4×4. It was now up to us to navigate back to Luanda. The usual crowd of children gathered as Alfy worked his magic, turning the Klepper from a pile of spare parts into the kayak that had carried us over such a long distance this past month. Over the course of 20 minutes, the Klepper came back to life as the river flowed lazily past in the background. Soon, we slipped back into the current and were swept away from the bank. It felt great to be back. No, it felt better than great. Finally, we allowed ourselves some hope: perhaps we would finish after all? Our new target: paddle out into the Atlantic Ocean by Wednesday 6 July.

Figure 31 – Garcia watches Alfy prep the Klepper to return to the river (3 July 2016)

Our re-entry point put us very close to the Cambambe Fort, which once housed one of Angola's most fascinating historical characters. For the rest of our journey we would be retracing the steps of Andrew Battel, an English pirate, adventurer and mercenary who lived in Angola between 1590 and 1606. Of course, back then it was not called Angola.

The geographic space that forms modern Angola was only brought under effective Portuguese control after the First World War. Before European arrival, Angola was divided into numerous distinct zones, each with their own kingdoms and cultures. The Kongo Kingdom, established in the late fourteenth century, was the most developed and well documented. It covered the modern-day northern Angolan Atlantic coastline, encompassing territory now in the Republic of Congo, Cabinda, the Democratic Republic of Congo and southern Gabon. However, our journey in the east of the country was taking us through areas once controlled by the Matamba, Imbangala Jagas and various Ovimbundu kingdoms of the central plateau such as Viye and Nudulu.

Battel was first brought to Luanda as a Portuguese prisoner, having been captured on an English pirate vessel near Rio de Janeiro, Brazil, in 1589. He spent the next 16 years moving up and down the Kwanza River trading and fighting (for both the Portuguese and the local

Imbangala Jagas warriors), as well as spending multiple periods in Portuguese custody. Battel lived and worked in Cambambe between 1604 and 1606, while the fort was being constructed by Portuguese Governor Manuel Cerveira Pereira.

That morning we also passed through Dondo, which is home to the Eka brewery, making one of Angola's most popular beers. We only covered 25km that Sunday, due to our late start. We were helped by a wide, fast river and the lack of hippos, rapids and waterfalls that we had been excited about ever since clearing Malanje Bridge. Our average speed towards the end of the day had shot up to 7.7kmph, a full 3kmph faster than some of the slower sections of the upper course. The speed of the water here was helping us a lot. On the other hand, our progress was hampered by a number of slow leaks in the Klepper, battle scars from previous encounters with rapids before the arrest.

That afternoon we paddled past Massangano, site of another sixteenth-century Portuguese fort. The square, white-brick construction offers commanding views over a vast stretch of the river. Andrew Battel was imprisoned here from 1591 to 1596, following an unsuccessful attempt to escape the Portuguese colony and return to England on a Dutch vessel. By now we could certainly empathise with Battel's struggles to escape the Portuguese bureaucracy.

David Livingstone also visited the town during his trans-continental expedition of 1854 to 1856. He disparagingly noted in his diary:

> Massangano was a very important town at the time the Dutch held forcible possession of Loanda [Luanda] and part of Angola; but when, in the year 1648, the Dutch were expelled from this country by a small body of Portuguese, under the Governor Salvador Correa de Sa Benevides, Massangano was left to sink into its present decay.

The colonial ruins overlooking the river were a chilling reminder of the brutal trade that the Kwanza River helped to bring to the heart of Angola. But they were also a reminder that we were getting ever closer to the former seat of Portuguese imperial power and our finish line: the coast around Luanda.

We paddled right up until dark, then found a root-covered bank to haul the Klepper up onto, out of sight from the surrounding river. The mosquitoes on this lower section of the river were unbearable. They appeared around dusk and stuck around for a good few hours, biting through multiple layers of our clothing. What a pain it would be to get malaria on this final section, but this was not a major threat to the expedition: given its incubation period, by the time the disease kicked in, we would be back in Luanda (if all went according to plan).

Knowing that we only had four days of expedition left, we had dumped a pile of gear and brought generous quantities of food. This changed the character of our expedition somewhat: there was much more of a sense of urgency, but less day-to-day hunger. The discomfort of dealing with my feet every evening had now been replaced with the discomfort of aching muscles and mosquito bites.

That night we cooked up a chorizo-based feast, so much in fact that we could not finish it! This was a first for the expedition.

On Monday, 4 July we were up at 5.30am, before sunrise. Alfy patched up the Klepper by torchlight, while two fires kept away the swarms of mosquitoes. The fires were invisible to the outside world, shielded by the dense trees surrounding our campsite. We shovelled down generous bowls of porridge and set off. We were going to need the energy: we had to break the 70km mark to remain on schedule.

We started well, hitting 8kmph as we glided along the wide, flat expanses of the lower section, with *imbondeiro* trees and white cliffs on both sides. At lunchtime, we hit the waterfront town of Muxima and stopped for a coffee.

Again, the nearby presence of settled communities on this stretch of the river completely changed our experience of the expedition. We felt safer, not simply due to the lack of hippos, but also as we were visibly less isolated.

Founded in 1599 by the Portuguese, Muxima was a key centre for slave traders. The church, known as *Nossa Senhora da Conceição da Muxima*, was used to baptise enslaved Angolans before they were shipped off to the New World down the Kwanza River. The sleepy town attracts hundreds of thousands of pilgrims from across the country for an annual religious ceremony in August and September, but outside this time, it feels very cut off from the rest of the country.

Alfy had visited one of the hotels here on his previous kayak journey with his brothers back in 2014. The owner was an eccentric Angolan-German, who had returned from Berlin full of ideas on how to turn his sleepy property into a tourist magnet. He was well placed to do so: the hotel could be reached on a day trip from the capital and offered scenic waterfront views.

From what we saw as we paddled up to his jetty, things had not gone as planned: the hotel's boat had sunk in the shallow water, and the only people using the riverside terrace were local women drying their clothes in the sun.

'This is unbelievable,' Alfy noted. 'Think how much money this owner could make, running day trips from Luanda up and down the river? I mean, it wouldn't take that much investment.'

After a quick coffee break, we jumped back in the Klepper and pushed on. The owner was nowhere to be seen.

With no hippos in the water and within driving distance from Luanda, we could risk it and paddle right up until sunset. That day we covered 72km, a new record. Everything was going according to plan: my feet were almost fully healed, we were setting a blistering pace and we had heard no indication that the authorities were out looking for us.

We made camp in a grove of banana trees right next to a village. Just as we were arriving, a long pirogue with an outboard motor came shooting past, carrying ten passengers. A few people waved. We had reached the easternmost extent of the busiest section of the river. It was now inhabited virtually the whole length to the Atlantic, barring the section that passed through Quiçama National Park. Our paranoia began to return. We needed to stay out of sight. We ducked into the foliage and set up our tents.

Just as we were setting up, an old man came walking out of one of the nearby fields. We asked him if it was OK to camp here.

'Here? Sure! But why would you want to? Do you know how many mosquitoes there are?' He walked off laughing, as we were slowly devoured by biting insects. Despite the tropical heat along this section, stopping for the night involved putting on as many layers as

Figure 32 – Paddling until sunset on the home stretch (4 July 2016)

possible, in a bid to prevent malaria or, worse yet, dengue fever. We lit a smoky fire and sat in front of it, the grey clouds washing over us.

'What are we going to do about the checkpoint at Bom Jesus tomorrow?' I asked.

'Good question! Our approach back in 2014 was to just ignore the police while they shouted at us from the river bank, pretend we hadn't seen them and push on.'

'And how did that work out for you?'

'Yeah, not great. Eventually they got in a patrol boat, chased us down and towed us back to the police station. The commander was absolutely furious. We just feigned ignorance and tried to talk him out of confiscating all our passports.'

We had to avoid this happening.

'It's only one or two guys in a boat. You can see them as you round one of the meanders just before Bom Jesus. Let's get there and play it by ear.'

On Tuesday, 5 July we were once again up before dawn. If all went according to plan, this would be our last dawn-to-dusk paddling session, culminating in us camping in Quiçama National Park. Then the next day it would only be a half day before we hit the Atlantic. The excitement was beginning to build.

We had a generally uneventful day of paddling. The river was very wide, and for some reason the flow rate completely dropped off in sections, leaving us really struggling to hit a good top speed. The extra calories we were carrying came in useful as we dug in with our paddles, dragging ourselves closer and closer to the final destination. However, we still had the issue of the police checkpoint at Bom Jesus to contend with.

We hit Bom Jesus just before 1pm, the twin chimney stacks of the abandoned Brazilian sugar factory coming into view on the horizon.

For all the time we had had to cook up a covert plan, this was the best we could come up with: sneak up to the police boat on the other side of the river in the reeds, then sprint past it as fast as possible, hoping they were all on their lunch break.

I reflected on video as we waited around the corner on the river: 'We are kind of hoping that we get to breeze through [Bom Jesus] with no issues and that the Chief of Police in Malanje, Mr Tony Bernardo, has not phoned ahead and told them to look out for two guys in a kayak.'

Alfy chimed in: 'I'm feeling optimistic. I'm also hoping, that if we get stopped, they don't open this video!'

We laughed at the thought, but it would not have been an amusing result. Luckily for us, our ridiculous plan worked. There was one policeman wandering around by some buildings back from the jetty, but the police boat was moored with no crew on board. Our heart rates shot up as we sprinted past the checkpoint, ducking low and trying not to splash with our paddles. We celebrated as we cleared the checkpoint.

On the other bank, water trucks loaded up to take their precious cargo into the *musseques* of Luanda, where they would sell it for up to $18 per cubic metre, according to the NGO Development Workshop. The informal water market supplies over 50 per cent of Luanda's water, in an industry worth $250 million per year. In this part of the country, the Kwanza River is big business, which explains the significant police presence.

We took our last afternoon on the water as an opportunity to reflect on the journey thus far and what we found most surprising about the whole experience (apart from the whole arrest issue).

Alfy went first: 'I have been really surprised by the sheer number of hippos on the upper stretches. I thought we would see a few, but had no idea that we would be dealing with them every day over such a long period of time.'

My main surprise had been the isolation. I thought that there would be communities on the river all the way along, trading and fishing. Many people had thought we would be able to buy fish and food on a regular basis and not have to be this self-sufficient on the rations front. On reflection, it made sense for communities to live back from the river due to the malaria risk, but the sheer absence of traffic on the water was amazing, especially considering the lack of roads or other transport arteries. It showed just how sparsely populated those parts of central Angola were.

The last 5km before we hit Quiçama National Park were brutal: a strong headwind picked up, stirring up large waves that crashed against the Klepper as it cut through the water. We had to dig in and really pull just to hit 4kmph. It was wet, windy and exhausting, but there was nothing that could dampen our spirits by this stage. We pushed on, knowing how close we were to a comfortable camping spot. As we passed a sign designating this stretch of the river as a protected manatee zone, we knew we had entered the national park. Finally, it was time to camp. We had covered 68km.

We moored at the national park jetty, which the rangers use to store their patrol boats. Occasionally, guides also use this mooring to take visitors out for tours of the river. If they are lucky, they will see a manatee, but more often than not it is a birding trip, with a few crocodiles thrown in for good measure. The mooring is at the foot of a large hill, which has a *jango* on top of it for viewing the river. Near the mooring is a small car park and a couple of shipping containers converted into park offices. A large white UNIMOG (a rugged all-wheel drive truck) was parked by one of the containers, along with a Ford Ranger, indicating that one of the park employees was still around.

As with entering Alfy's flat a few nights beforehand, it felt odd climbing out of the kayak into Quiçama National Park. This was a place that I was intimately familiar with, having visited numerous times throughout my life in Luanda. But it all felt different now, alien in some way. Again, we had a sense that we were intruders, that we did not belong here.

The heavy Klepper made a lot of noise as it was hauled out of the water, and sure enough, a man soon appeared from the offices to see what was going on. Alex introduced himself as the chief ranger in that sector. In his late fifties, his muscular build and well-kept uniform hinted at his military past. We asked if it was OK to camp and he radioed his supervisor to ask, before confirming that we were fine for the night. We invited him to join us for dinner by the fire that I was busy lighting.

We spent our last night on the Kwanza sharing chorizo, rice and even a marshmallow dessert with Alex, as he told us stories of fighting for the MPLA during the civil war. He was appreciative of the job he now had, as all national park roles in this province were reserved for military veterans. However, he complained about the terrible inflation eating into his purchasing power. His monthly salary was now hardly enough to buy a 10kg bag of rice, and he had a large family to support back in Luanda. Occasionally, he would break from our conversation to shine a high-powered torch out onto the river.

'We must be vigilant all night. The poachers try and sneak in to hunt the manatees, right in front of us when it is dark.'

Alex was the only line of defence that night between all of Quiçama's animals and poachers coming in from the river. The elephants, manatee, zebra, giraffe, ostriches and wildebeest were all reliant on him to keep them safe that evening. The park is also home to hippos, but only in the Longa River to the south. There were none left in this section of the Kwanza due to poaching during the civil war. Now things have changed and conservation is a focus of the Angolan government. Now skilled, dedicated citizens like Alex work hard to protect nature for very little money in these difficult and isolated locations.

Eventually Alex said goodnight and walked back up the hill, leaving us alone by the river, toasting our marshmallows. This was it. Our last night camping on the Kwanza. The beginning of the expedition felt like it was a lifetime ago.

It was hard to remember what my expectations had been for this trip as I lay there in my tent by the river's source, 32 days earlier. Had we always been confident we would finish? Perhaps I had not. Despite the arrest and the foot injury and the sinking, looking back, I told Alfy that the only time I genuinely worried we would not reach this point was on day three, when my back did not seem up to the task. Alfy admitted that for him, the lowest point came much later, while sat in the deportation centre in Viana.

Wednesday, 6 July was scheduled as the last day of the expedition. Our morning began with a walk up to the *jango* overlooking the river to send messages to everyone in Luanda to expect our arrival at the Kwanza Lodge that afternoon. Kwanza Lodge is a South African-run fishing lodge right on the mouth of the river. We were already salivating at the thought of arriving there: they had an all-you-can-eat buffet and ice-cold beers. The perfect finish line.

Before our well-deserved meal, we had to tackle the final 40km of the Kwanza River. The beginning of the day was spent winding our way through Quiçama. The jungle canopy stretched all the way to the banks, and often out into the river itself, collapsed palm trees forming natural obstacles on either side.

Monkeys shrieked in dismay as we paddled past, chasing us through the treetops until we were off their patch. The only access to the banks were from the trails elephants and warthogs had trampled in the foliage to the water's edge. Crocodiles watched us move past, only occasionally bothering to slither into the water due to our presence. This was a pleasant way to while away the time as we inched ever closer to the finish line.

At 11.20am we hit the Kwanza Bridge, a landmark Alfy and I knew well. Any time we wanted to go surfing along Angola's southern coastline, we would drive over this bridge, which is only 45 minutes south of Luanda. The bridge is 4km inland and home to a pack of monkeys that have learned to steal food out of cars slowing for the speed bumps. We were less than an hour away from the finish line.

The final stretch became progressively more difficult due to an onshore wind blowing up a lot of chop on the river. By the time we passed the last bend, we were faced with 1km of open water and then

Kwanza Lodge, sat on the Atlantic coast. We pushed forwards as the wind blew harder and harder.

Waves splashed into the top of the kayak. I could feel my feet getting wet as we took on water.

'Wouldn't it be embarrassing to sink within sight of the finish line?'

I did not answer. We would swim if we had to and drag the boat out later. We had to make it. My mind cast back to previous visits to Kwanza Lodge and the size of the crocodiles sunning themselves on the beach there. The river mouth is also home to bull sharks.

Figure 33 – Stood in the Atlantic Ocean, 1,300km from where we started (6 July 2016). Image credit: Marie-Louise Henham

On the Kwanza Lodge's jetty, we could see Marie-Louise, waving an Angolan flag and cheering loudly. Next to her, our German friend Jörg, Alfy's former housemate Joost and two representatives from the HALO Trust, as well as Manny, the South African manager of the lodge. We paddled past them, out to a sand spit that stretched across the river mouth. Clambering out of the Klepper, we carried it the last 100m into the Atlantic Ocean and placed it down in the water. Marie-Louise and the gang were following in the Kwanza Lodge's fishing boat, filming the final moments of the expedition. The waves were crashing around us as we waded into the ocean, waist deep. We unfolded an Angolan flag and waved it wildly. We had made it. Our Kwanza expedition was complete.

Epilogue

Alfy and I had kayaked 984km on an independent, self-propelled journey of over 1,300km. Stood on the jetty of Kwanza Lodge, waiting for our all-you-can-eat celebratory buffet to be ready, we reflected on some of the difficulties we had faced for those who had gathered to see us.

Jörg, ever the fitness enthusiast, focused on the endurance requirements of the expedition. Joost, having worked previously on safaris in Southern Africa, was keen to hear more about the dangerous wildlife. Marie-Louise was just pleased to have Alfy back in one piece and was not as shocked as everyone else at how much weight we had lost (after all, she had been with us only four days before). Marie-Louise also updated us on how our various family members and loved ones were doing, given our period of radio silence. Alfy's father in particular was relieved that we were finally off the river.

José Pedro Agostinho, known as Zeca, was the most senior HALO Trust representative on the finish line. He is Angola's Deputy Programme Manager, and he started by expressing his gratitude for our fundraising efforts. Zeca had brought us all new branded HALO Trust polo shirts for some promotional photographs. It was not until Alfy and I peeled off our old ones, which had been worn continuously for a month, that we realised how sun bleached and filthy they were.

After eating, taking photos and dismantling the Klepper for the last time by the side of the river, we headed back to Luanda in Joost's 4×4.

Alfy hosted a rooftop party at his flat overlooking Chicala to celebrate finishing. He even assembled the Klepper on the roof to show all the guests the kayak we had been sat in for the better part of a month. As the school summer holidays had now begun, none of my teacher friends at Luanda International School were in the country, which was a shame, but we still managed a good turnout. We stood on the roof, drinks in hand, watching the sunset over the futuristic Neto Mausoleum, which looks like a 120m-high space rocket. These cosmopolitan surroundings were a jarring contrast to our recent river environment.

Alfy was thrust straight back into the office. He now only had a few days before the handover and there was a great deal to be organised. Before flying back to Europe, I spent one afternoon surfing at Cabo Ledo with Jörg, who had promised to take me if we made it back in one piece. His dogs, two massive German Shepherds, spent the whole time running out into the sea chasing us.

Every wave I dropped down felt fantastic: to be in the water, having fun, with no safety concerns. It was cleansing. There were no hippos or crocodiles here.

After catching a few waves, I just lay on my surfboard in the water, looking up at the sky. The fresh smell of the ocean contrasting with the musty, often dank aromas from the river.

It took me a while to recover once I got back to the UK. I was thrilled to see Steph after 46 days apart. It was our longest period away from each other in our four-year relationship. I saw my mother and brother again, thanking them for all their support. My mind cast back to Alfy's comments out on the water: how journeys like these are an inherently selfish act and how much they ask of the loved ones that you leave behind.

London was too busy, too crowded. I longed for the silence of the river and the structure of the paddling day. I missed the dead silence of the night times and the evening grunts of the hippos, now replaced with the familiar sirens and hustle of a modern city. Two of my fingernails had a fungal infection from getting so much filthy river water under them and were threatening to drop off. Soon, after ignoring the problem, it was eight fingernails.

My close friends organised a kitesurfing trip down to the coast in Rye, West Sussex, to catch up and celebrate. That first evening I drank one rum and coke and vomited: my body was not used to alcohol. One enduring memory from that evening in our rented cottage was a speech given by my close friend David, while Dan and Jonathan sipped their pints.

We have all known each other since secondary school and grew up together, although we ended up on very different paths. David was an officer in the Parachute Regiment, before working for the HALO Trust and finally the Foreign and Commonwealth Office. Dan was

Epilogue

now a chartered quantity surveyor in London, while we all liked to joke that nobody was quite sure what Jonathan did. Something in finance in London.

David said that they were all very proud and that they had been constantly checking the live-updated map to follow our progress. David never had any doubt that we would finish. It was touching, almost overwhelming, although I did not say so at the time.

The reception our expedition received upon completion was greater than we had ever imagined. Over twenty-five thousand dollars were donated to the HALO Trust, which funded the deployment of two demining teams down in Cuito Cuanavale for a month. Together, they cleared 18,520m^2 of mined ground of high humanitarian priority, which was then returned to the local population for productive use. The HALO Trust teams destroyed 121 anti-personnel mines and 93 anti-tank mines, as well as two items of unexploded ordnance (UXO) of calibre greater than 20mm. The documentary film we made of the journey was aired in film festivals in Cyprus, the USA, the UK, Canada and Australia, helping to publicise the HALO Trust's vital work internationally. On 22 March 2017 I had the honour of being invited to give a lecture at The Royal Geographical Society in London as part of their 'Microlectures' series on geographical journeys.

Alfy and I have only seen each other once since that journey. He jetted off to Hong Kong to start his new job. I have since moved to Madagascar to start mine. We have made vague plans to see each other in South Africa at some stage. Perhaps we will even start plotting another adventure.

My mind often drifts back to our time on the river. How privileged we were to see such a hidden side of life in rural Angola: the *soba* mediations, the camaraderie in the diamond mines, the fishermen and subsistence farmers scratching out a living in that hostile and ancient environment. We were welcomed and assisted by the vast majority of the people we met, and for this both Alfy and I are eternally thankful. We could never have finished without all the direction and advice that we received from the Angolan people. In fact, we could very well have ended up like those two South African kayakers who lost their lives near the Capanda Dam.

I am also saddened by some of what we saw: the destructive wildfires, miners dredging the river, bulldozing roads into the wilderness of the Bié Plateau. The poverty of some of those mining camps, a jarring contrast to the wealth they were pulling out of the ground.

What stuck with me most of all was the arbitrary fashion in which power is often wielded in the Angolan state. We were very lucky: a detention of only four days and no physical abuse is far better treatment than many of those detained by the security services receive. The Angolan people do not have professional diplomats to intervene on their behalf as we did.

To this day we still do not know exactly why we were released from that detention centre or if we now have criminal records in Angola. Alfy and I wrote to Carlos, David and Gianluca to thank them for their assistance, but our correspondence provided no clarity. The four-day interruption messed up our world record attempt and is still proving difficult to square with the Guinness World Record authorities.

One day I would like to return to Angola, return to the Luando Nature Reserve, but not rush through this time. Appreciate the wilderness with functioning feet and a little less codeine in my system. Perhaps track down that lion, or even some of the Palancas. In the meantime, I am pleased that there are people like Alex and Pedro Vaz Pinto conserving the environment and that the HALO Trust is slowly making it safe again, for all of Angola's citizens to enjoy.

London, June 2017

Appendix 1 – A very brief history of Angola

Angola has a troubled history with outsiders. Over the past six centuries, it has been the scene of exploitation and conflict, which often dominates international discourse on the country. Angola is also a nation of extreme contrasts, and it was my home from 2009 to 2014.

It is beyond the scope of this book to delve too deeply into the complex pre-colonial and colonial history of Angola or how this fed into the post-independence conflict. Suffice to say that from the moment Portuguese explorer Diogo Cão arrived at the mouth of the Congo (modern Soyo) on 23 April 1483 until independence on 11 November 1975, Angola was forged into an increasingly divided society which was unlikely to be viable upon the departure of the colonial power.

Between 1961 and 1974 the Angolan people fought a war of independence against the colonial Portuguese authorities. Upon independence in 1975, a brutal civil war broke out that lasted until 2002. Any Angolan born before 1988 has spent the majority of their life in a country at war. Those born after 1979 only ever knew one political leader: President Jose Eduardo dos Santos (until his retirement in September 2017). His predecessor, the respected independence leader Agostinho Neto, lasted less than four years in the top role before succumbing to cancer in a Moscow hospital in September 1979.

The Portuguese colonial economy in Angola was one based on extraction, whether this was slaves, ivory, agricultural products or, later, oil and diamonds. Ethnic divisions were exacerbated through deliberate colonial policy. Slave traders sent up to 3 million Angolans and Congolese across the Atlantic to work on the plantations of the New World, especially in Brazil. Angolans were still harvesting Cadbury's cocoa on the nearby island plantations of São Tomé in slave-like conditions in 1907 (despite Portugal having ostensibly abolished the trade in 1836). In Angola itself, forced labour remained a central pillar of the colonial economy until reforms in 1962.

Figure 34 – Former Portuguese cocoa plantation, São Tomé (June 2014)

The Portuguese authorities liked to present their rule as benevolent and civilising. Under the banner of 'Lusotropicalism', they highlighted the multicultural nature of Angolan society which they felt made their colonies more racially democratic than those of other European powers.

In reality, this was a deeply racist and exploitative regime that afforded a small European and even smaller native *Assimilado* or *mestiço* population a quality of life that would be difficult to sustain back in Portugal. Luanda was a shining cultural capital of the Lusophone world, with the latest fashions and music often hitting Luanda's streets before Lisbon's. This elite lifestyle came at the expense of the vast majority of Angolans, many of whom were exploited through forced labour until the early 1960s.

Portugal itself suffered under a fascist dictatorship known as the Estado Novo between 1933 and 1974, so it is unsurprising that colonial authority in Angola was based on the widespread use of violence and that Africa's 'wind of change' of the 1960s took rather longer to reach Portuguese colonies than those of other more democratic European powers.

It is also no surprise that one of the earliest centres of resistance was Malanje Province, a cotton-producing region in the east that we planned to kayak through in the last third of our journey. Malanje suffered brutal forced-labour practices to get goods to the international market as cheaply as possible. Bringing the full force of the Portuguese military to bear against these rebellious farming communities, the colonial authorities had killed up to 40,000 Angolans in this province by March 1961 to try to put down the uprising, sometimes using napalm to destroy whole villages.

In the end, Angolan independence came as the result of political changes back in Portugal, rather than the military defeat of the occupying colonial forces. From 1961 onwards, the Estado Novo found itself fighting a grinding war of attrition against guerrillas in all of its African colonies (Mozambique, Guinea-Bissau and Angola). This *Guerra do Ultramar* (Overseas War) was likened to Portugal's version of Vietnam, sucking up almost 40 per cent of government spending and killing over 8,000 troops. With funds and morale back home being sapped and no end in sight, on 25 April 1974 a bloodless military coup was launched in Lisbon (the Carnation Revolution). It was led by low-ranking Portuguese army officers, who wanted to stop the *Guerra do Ultramar* as soon as possible and return Portugal to democracy. Lisbon's iconic suspension bridge over the Tagus river is named after this event.

Having seized power, the officers implemented one of the fastest decolonisation programmes on the continent, propelling Angola from an overseas province of Portugal to an independent nation-state in just 18 months.

The Portuguese departure from Angola was more of a panicked evacuation than a structured decolonisation. Before the Carnation Revolution in 1974, an estimated 500,000 Portuguese settlers were living in Angola. By July 1975, 6,000 people a week were jumping on commercial flights out of Angola, with another 3,500 fleeing on Portuguese military aircraft. This mass exodus of skilled labour, known as the *retornados* back in the mother country, brought the Angolan economy to the brink of collapse. In one final dereliction of responsibility, on the evening of 10 November, the Portuguese High Commissioner in Luanda, Admiral Leonel Cardoso, handed over sovereignty to 'the Angolan people', rather than transferring power to one of the three competing liberation movements. He then unceremoniously fled to the harbour, an ignoble end to five centuries of Portuguese colonial rule.

The United States and many Western nations supported invading South African troops as they tried to install a National Union for the Total Independence of Angola (*União Nacional para a Independência Total de Angola*: UNITA) government into this power vacuum from 1975. The UNITA movement, led by the charismatic Jonas Savimbi, took an anti-communist stance in a part of Africa that the West was concerned was at high-risk of a communist takeover. Savimbi drew much of his support from Angola's majority Ovimbundu ethnic group, who are concentrated on the Bié Plateau, an area we would be travelling through extensively on our expedition.

This stage of the Angolan Civil War famously featured 32 Battalion. They were an elite group of South African soldiers who enjoyed incredible success on the battlefield under the command of Colonel Jan Breytenbach, until they were disbanded after Apartheid ended. Some of these former soldiers would later go on to play significant roles in the infamous private military company, Executive Outcomes, as well as being involved in the alleged coup attempt by Simon Mann in Equatorial Guinea in 2004. Leonardo di Caprio's character in the 2006 thriller *Blood Diamond*, about a Rhodesian gun-runner during the civil war in Sierra Leone, was loosely based on a real member of 32 Battalion. He even talks about his time in Angola in the film.

The rival People's Movement for the Liberation of Angola (*Movimento Popular de Libertação de Angola*: MPLA), more naturally aligned with the communist bloc, was immediately supported by an influx of 25,000 Cuban troops upon independence in November 1975. These incoming troops helped to rout a National Front for the Liberation of Angola (*Frente Nacional de Libertação de Angola*: FNLA) invasion from neighbouring Zaire on 10 November 1975, ending any realistic hopes they had of seizing power. From then on, the civil war was a two-horse race: UNITA versus the MPLA.

Fidel Castro saw it as his duty to support the fledgling communist state and also to prevent the spread of the Apartheid government northwards from South West Africa (modern-day Namibia), which was at that time a South African mandate. While the Soviet Union was initially reluctant to get involved, Fidel Castro's unilateral intervention forced their hand, and eventually the Soviets became heavily committed to supporting the MPLA's war effort with military equipment, intelligence support and funding. The Cubans also helped to prop up independent Angola's civil service by sending doctors, teachers and engineers to fill the gap left by the departing Portuguese colonists.

As the Cold War ended, South African and Cuban troops withdrew from the Angolan theatre. An internationally brokered ceasefire, the Bicesse Accords, was signed in 1991, with elections held in 1992. However, these broke down before completion, with UNITA rejecting the results of the first round. This left the MPLA and UNITA to settle their differences alone on the battlefield, with Western nations gradually withdrawing their support for UNITA. As the war restarted in late 1992, UNITA scored a stunning series of victories to control 70 per cent of the country by the end of 1993 (including almost the entire course of the Kwanza River), and relegating the MPLA to control of inland provincial capitals and sections of the coast (including Luanda). This period saw some of the most brutal fighting of the whole civil war and accounted for at least 60 per cent of the total casualties. Over 20 million landmines were planted. It would take the MPLA another 10 years of conflict to regain control of the country.

Most civil wars in Africa since 1991 have tended to end in a messy foreign-brokered peace settlement. In Angola, the current government, the MPLA, won undisputed power in 2002 by inflicting a crushing military defeat on UNITA, killing UNITA's long-time leader Jonas Savimbi in the process. Since then, the ruling party has faced few political or economic obstacles to reconstructing the devastated Angolan society in whatever manner they saw fit, with Luanda as its glistening centrepiece.

The legacy of the civil war is never far away if you are willing to venture outside the capital. To leave Luanda and drive into the interior of Angola is to enter another world. This world would be far more in keeping with the often-inaccurate Western media stereotypes of Africa: widespread poverty, tropical diseases, burned-out tanks, minefields.

Before I moved to Angola in 2009, few of my friends in the UK knew much about it. There might have been the odd newspaper headline on growing oil output or government corruption, but it was not a place that figured highly on the international news agenda. The older generation might be able to tell me something about a long-running civil war, or 'that rebel leader Savimbi' as one taxi driver put it, but again, this was an opaque space in most people's understanding of the continent.

In contrast to this, the Portuguese people I spoke to had much more to say. The place was an economic miracle, an incredible land of abundant natural resources and almost limitless potential. But it had been much better run under the Portuguese. Since decolonisation in 1975, the locals had messed everything up. Why did they have to fight?

One friend, João, based in the south of Portugal, looked dejectedly at me as I asked him about Angola one summer. Being much older than me, he had seen Angola under Portuguese colonial rule.

'Mozambique, Bissau, Timor-Leste, you can keep them. But Angola... we should never have given that place up. It could have really been something.'

In some ways, I agreed with João. Angola was not just a passive backdrop to our kayaking expedition. Angola was my home for five years and Alfy's for three. I loved the place.

Luanda saw little actual fighting during the long civil war. There were a series of massacres and running street battles when the internationally brokered elections broke down in October and November 1992, but generally speaking the city remained peaceful throughout the 27-year conflict. Your main clue as to what happened outside the city comes from the odd historic monument or the streets themselves, which often bear the names of heroic wartime commanders. The dark recent past is not a natural topic of conversation with foreigners, beyond acknowledging that things are much better now and nobody wants to go back to the *confusão* of that period.

Angola's first oil-backed loans from China were rolled out in March 2004, and from then on, Angola was the scene of rapid reconstruction, development and consumption, with Luanda at its epicentre. Angolan citizens have watched their post-war economy grow tenfold, from $12.49 billion in 2002 to $126.77 billion in 2014. With billions of dollars flowing in from the Chinese and no questions asked about transparency or accountability, things had never been better for Luanda's urban elite. Western oil majors such as Total, Chevron and BP also pumped billions into the economy to extract Angola's precious oil. Over the past 13 years, Angola's oil generated an income of $468 billion, dwarfing foreign aid flows to the entire continent. Official development assistance for Africa stood at only $91 billion for the same time period, according to the OECD. This wealth gave the victorious MPLA carte blanche to pursue the policy objectives of their choice, with little reliance on outside funding, approval or oversight.

Every year the human resources consulting firm, Mercer, publishes a ranking of global cities, based on the cost of living for expatriate workers. Between 2010 and 2016, Luanda was the most expensive city on the list five times. It was only knocked into second place by Tokyo in 2012 and Hong Kong in 2016. Glossy government images show the high-rise-lined waterfront Marginal, or the opulent clubs and bars with their own private beaches along the Ilha. Here you can enjoy hundred-dollar 'boats' of sushi while listening to famous Brazilian or Portuguese DJs. Out in the harbour, private yacht owners have access to some of the best sport fishing in the region. I saw more than a few Ferraris in my time there.

Another South African friend who worked in Luanda's construction boom, lived in an exclusive gated compound in the southern residential suburb of Talatona. He observed a fascinating ritual one weekend in 2011 that showed the lengths people were willing to go to engage in conspicuous consumption. His neighbour, a wealthy Angolan, had a series of luxury sports cars parked on his driveway, including a brand-new Lamborghini. The problem was, the compound was dotted with massive speed bumps to protect the children on the estate from speeding vehicles. Given the poor wheel clearance of most Lamborghinis, this left his car effectively stranded, unable to drive out of the compound. Not to be deterred, the owner simply had a tow truck turn up whenever he wanted to take the car out for a spin, hoist the vehicle onto the back, drive out of the compound then deposit it on the road outside. The whole operation had to be repeated in reverse to get it back inside at the end of the jaunt.

Luanda is a financial anomaly: a sub-Saharan African city with rental prices higher than London or New York. My two-bedroom apartment cost my employer nine thousand dollars a month, and this was by no means luxurious. Power cuts and water shortages were regular features of Luandan living. A lack of basic infrastructure, no manufacturing base and a series of monopolies on the import market made everything eye-wateringly expensive. I learned this the hard way during the first week in the country: accidentally paying twenty-four dollars for a four-pack of yoghurt as I had neglected to check the price. In truth, the financial haemorrhaging started well before I arrived in-country. My economy British Airways flight from London to Luanda (8.5 hours direct) set me back £1,935. Unlike the majority of other people on that plane, I did not work in the oil industry. I was heading to Angola to teach History at Luanda International School.

Appendix 2 – Equipment list

Watercraft and peripherals

- Klepper Aerius II 545 Classic two-man collapsible kayak
- Werner Cyprus carbon-fibre paddle – 220cm (Oscar's paddle)
- Werner Shuna carbon-fibre paddle – 230cm (Alfy's paddle)
- Werner Tybee fibreglass reinforced nylon paddle – 230cm (backup paddle)
- Lifejackets
- Jackson Sweet Cheeks inflatable kayak seats
- Lomo 15m kayak throwline

Electronics

- Garmin GPS Map 64
- Thuraya SO-2510 satellite phone
- Nokia 105 mobile phone
- Iridium 9555 satellite phone
- Samsung Galaxy SIII smartphone
- Voltaic Systems 17 Watt solar charger kit
- Voltaic V72 battery
- Canon Legria HF 606 HD video camera
- Canon EOS 450d DSLR camera
- DJI Phantom 3 Standard drone
- GoPro Hero HD surf camera and waterproof case
- LED Lenser SEO7R Rechargeable Li-ion Head Torch

Bags and Storage

- Nanuk 904 Waterproof Case
- Osprey Atmos AG 65 backpack
- Ortlieb 79L drybags
- Ziploc food bags
- The Scrubba wash and drybag

Cooking

- Cape Union Mart Blue Sky Tuffware Utensil set (cutlery)
- Lixada wood burning stove
- Trangia series 27 stove
- Water-to-Go 750ml water filtration bottles
- Sawyer Squeeze Mini Water Filtration System
- Wet Ones
- Blackhawk! antimicrobial hydration reservoir kit (100oz)
- CamelBak Antidote reservoir (3 litres)

Camping

- OUTAD folding aluminium camp stool
- Banshee 200 tent
- Wild Country Zephyros I tent
- Therm-a-Rest NeoAir Xlite camping mat
- Therm-a-Rest NeoAir Venture camping mat
- Leatherman Kick multi-tool
- CRKT hunting knife
- Camillus X Carnivore machete
- Gerber knife sharpener
- EXPED Air Pillow
- Vango Ultralite 300 sleeping bag

Clothing

- Icebreaker Merino wool base layer
- North Face fleeces
- Cargo trousers
- Long-sleeve shirt
- Waterproof socks
- HALO Trust polo shirts, t-shirts, hats and caps
- Board shorts
- Neoprene gloves
- LifeSystems mosquito headnet
- Buff (neck gaiter)
- Bodhi microfiber travel towels
- Brasher Hillmaster II walking boots

Miscellaneous

- Compass
- Gorilla duct tape
- Gorilla superglue
- 550 paracord
- HAMA Star 61 tripod

Dehydrated rations

- Macaroni
- Apple and blueberry oats
- PG Tips teabags
- Mixed nuts
- Oat bran
- Coconut powder
- Peanuts
- Flavoured oat bars
- Snickers bars
- Couscous
- Wild rice
- Tomato soup
- Minestrone, chicken and vegetable soups
- Cheddar cheese sauce mix
- Beef stock cubes
- Chicken stock cubes
- Marmite
- Nutella
- Tabasco sauce
- Orange and pineapple squash
- Apple and blackcurrant squash
- Cod liver oil
- Glucosamine tablets
- Garlic
- Protein and creatine mix
- Hot chocolate
- Dried skimmed milk
- Nescafe coffee
- Cane sugar
- Pumpkin bark
- Kidney beans

- Bolognese with sriracha
- Tuna
- Pineapple
- Sweet potato bark
- Dried fish sticks

Appendix 3 – Medical gear

Essentials

- Zinc oxide tape
- Ibuprofen
- Coartem antimalarials
- Malaria testing kits
- Imodium (Loperamide)
- Betadine
- Gauze dressing
- Scissors
- Tweezers
- Latex gloves
- Condoms (useful in all sorts of situations!)
- Rehydration sachets
- Compeed blister pads
- Sterile saline eye wash
- Assorted syringes and needles (both for injecting your own stuff and handing over for use on you in poorly equipped local hospitals)
- Emergency dental filling and dental tools (mirror/plaque scraper)
- Multivitamins
- Dental floss

Analgesia

- Morphine/Ketamine (good luck getting these in Europe!)
- IM Voltarol (diclofenac)
- Rectal Voltarol (diclofenac)
- Co-codamol
- Paracetamol

Fracture management

- Various tapes (including Gorilla Tape)
- Clingfilm

- SAM Splints

Antibiotics

- Doxycycline (some prefer Malarone as an antimalarial)
- Co-Amoxiclav
- Ciprofloxacin
- Metronidazole
- Flucloxacillin

Creams, sprays and stuff to sort skin problems

- Clotrimazole antifungal cream
- Oto-Synalar N (Fluocinolone Acetonide) drops – for ear infections from water contact
- Cetirizine antihistamine
- Eurax cream for bites
- 1 per cent Hydrocortisone steroid cream
- Fucidin antibiotic cream
- Cetrimide antiseptic spray
- Daktarin (miconazole) spray
- Praziquantel (Biltricide) – for schistosomiasis (bilharzia)
- Burnshield Hydrogel

Dressings and wound closure

- Celox RAPID Z-Folded Haemostatic Gauze – 1.5m, for serious bleeds
- Simple dry dressings
- Tegaderm +Pads
- Plasters
- Tampons
- Crepe bandages for sling
- Steristrips
- Gorilla superglue
- Ethicon Mersilk suture kit and injectable local anaesthetic

Medical emergencies

- Treatment for anaphylaxis: adrenaline (Epinephrine), chlorpheniramine and hydrocortisone
- Oropharyngeal airway
- Tourniquets

IV Access and fluids

- IV Fluids
- Giving sets
- Venflons

Appendix 4 – Glossary and abbreviations

Chefe	Literally 'chief', used as a label for any hierarchical superior within the Angolan bureaucracy.
DEET	Diethyltoluamide is a strong insect repellent, originally developed for use by the US Army in the 1940s.
FAA	*Forças Armadas Angolanas* (Angolan Armed Forces)
FNLA	*Frente Nacional de Libertação de Angola* (The National Liberation Front of Angola). The oldest of Angola's national liberation movements. Played a significant role during the Angolan War of Independence (1961–1974) but has since become a marginalised opposition party.
Funge	A plain carbohydrate made from cassava flour (*fufu*), with the same consistency as mashed potato.
Garimpeiros	An artisanal diamond prospector, often working illegally.
INAD	*Instituto Nacional de Desminagem* (National Institute of Demining).
Jango	A communal thatched hut with open sides, usually in the centre of a village.
Kizomba	A genre of Angolan dance music, from the Kimbundu word for 'party'.
Makoro	A dugout canoe, often used in Botswana's Okavango Delta.
MPLA	*Movimento Popular de Libertação de Angola* (Popular Movement for the Liberation of Angola), the main national liberation movement and ruling party of Angola since independence.
Portage	Carrying a watercraft overland to avoid obstacles.
Soba	A traditional community leader.
UNITA	*União Nacional para a Independência Total de Angola* (The National Union for the Total Independence of Angola), a rival national liberation movement and main opponent of the MPLA during the Angolan Civil War. Now the main opposition party in Angola.

Patrons

Claudia Bartlett
Erin Blass
Samuel Bretzmann
Alasdair Campbell
Andy Coates
Olivia-Petra Coman
Katja Dannecker
Sarah Davis
Karen Drozdiak
David & Sara Elizalde
Ameria Farha
Lizzy Forster
Matthew Gelfand
Allison Gerns
Alan Griffith
Tom Hartnett
Sintija Jakane & Stéphane Bauvet
Richard Mallinson
Bob Mark
Aongus McGreal
Adam Moore
Carlo Navato
David Oliver
Olawale Opayinka
Ignacio Otaegui Satrústegui
David Pett
Tim Precious-Li
Timothy Prueter & Chloe Edwards
F Randle
Richard Reilly
Mark Richardson
Martin Roberts

Johannes Rutgers
Jessie Scott
Sean Stevenson
Rogier van der Sluijs
Clare Ward
Alfy Weston
Martin Wicks